Introduction t Personal Computers

Student Manual

Australia • Canada • Mexico • Singapore
Spain • United Kingdom • United States

Introduction to Personal Computers

VP and GM of Courseware:	Michael Springer
Series Product Managers:	Charles G. Blum and Adam A. Wilcox
Developmental Editor:	Leslie Caico
Copyeditor:	Geraldine Martin
Keytester:	Bill Bateman
Series Designer:	Adam A. Wilcox
Cover Designer:	Abby Scholz

COPYRIGHT © 2006 Course Technology, a division of Thomson Learning. Thomson Learning is a trademark used herein under license.

ALL RIGHTS RESERVED. No part of this work may be reproduced, transcribed, or used in any form or by any means—graphic, electronic, or mechanical, including photocopying, recording, taping, Web distribution, or information storage and retrieval systems—without the prior written permission of the publisher.

For more information contact:

Course Technology
25 Thomson Place
Boston, MA 02210

Or find us on the Web at: www.course.com

For permission to use material from this text or product, submit a request online at: www.thomsonrights.com

Any additional questions about permissions can be submitted by e-mail to: thomsonrights@thomson.com

Trademarks

Course ILT is a trademark of Course Technology.

Some of the product names and company names used in this book have been used for identification purposes only and may be trademarks or registered trademarks of their respective manufacturers and sellers.

Cover photograph courtesy of NASA (www.nasa.gov)

Disclaimer

Course Technology reserves the right to revise this publication and make changes from time to time in its content without notice.

ISBNs

1-4188-9056-1 = Student Manual

1-4188-9058-8 = Student Manual with data CD and CBT

Printed in the United States of America

1 2 3 4 5 6 7 8 9 PM 08 07 06

Contents

Introduction   iii

Topic A: About the manual iv
Topic B: Setting your expectations vii
Topic C: Re-keying the course ix

Introduction to computers   1-1

Topic A: Overview of computers 1-2
Topic B: How computers work 1-8
Topic C: Starting a computer 1-15
Unit summary: Introduction to computers 1-18

Input devices   2-1

Topic A: Mouse and keyboard basics 2-2
Topic B: Other input devices 2-7
Unit summary: Input devices 2-10

Processing data   3-1

Topic A: The system unit and the CPU 3-2
Topic B: Memory 3-6
Unit summary: Processing data 3-8

Data storage   4-1

Topic A: Floppy disks 4-2
Topic B: Hard disks 4-6
Topic C: Other storage devices 4-10
Unit summary: Data storage 4-14

Output devices   5-1

Topic A: Monitor and desktop layout basics 5-2
Topic B: Other output devices 5-7
Unit summary: Output devices 5-10

Managing data   6-1

Topic A: Working with Windows Explorer 6-2
Topic B: Working with folders 6-6
Topic C: Working with files 6-8
Topic D: Protecting data against viruses 6-20
Unit summary: Managing data 6-21

Working with applications   7-1

Topic A: Windows XP Accessories 7-2
Topic B: Outlook Express 7-11
Topic C: Internet Explorer 6.0 7-18
Topic D: Accessing Help and shutting down Windows XP 7-23
Unit summary: Working with applications 7-28

Course summary   S-1

Topic A: Course summary S-2

Introduction to Personal Computers

Topic B: Continued learning after class S-4

Quick reference   Q-1

Glossary   G-1

Index   I-1

Introduction

After reading this introduction, you will know how to:

A Use Course Technology ILT manuals in general.

B Use prerequisites, a target student description, course objectives, and a skills inventory to properly set your expectations for the course.

C Re-key this course after class.

Topic A: About the manual

Course Technology ILT philosophy

Course Technology ILT manuals facilitate your learning by providing structured interaction with the software itself. While we provide text to explain difficult concepts, the hands-on activities are the focus of our courses. By paying close attention as your instructor leads you through these activities, you will learn the skills and concepts effectively.

We believe strongly in the instructor-led classroom. During class, focus on your instructor. Our manuals are designed and written to facilitate your interaction with your instructor, and not to call attention to manuals themselves.

We believe in the basic approach of setting expectations, delivering instruction, and providing summary and review afterwards. For this reason, lessons begin with objectives and end with summaries. We also provide overall course objectives and a course summary to provide both an introduction to and closure on the entire course.

Manual components

The manuals contain these major components:

- Table of contents
- Introduction
- Units
- Course summary
- Quick reference
- Glossary
- Index

Each element is described below.

Table of contents

The table of contents acts as a learning roadmap.

Introduction

The introduction contains information about our training philosophy and our manual components, features, and conventions. It contains target student, prerequisite, objective, and setup information for the specific course.

Units

Units are the largest structural component of the course content. A unit begins with a title page that lists objectives for each major subdivision, or topic, within the unit. Within each topic, conceptual and explanatory information alternates with hands-on activities. Units conclude with a summary comprising one paragraph for each topic, and an independent practice activity that gives you an opportunity to practice the skills you've learned.

The conceptual information takes the form of text paragraphs, exhibits, lists, and tables. The activities are structured in two columns, one telling you what to do, the other providing explanations, descriptions, and graphics.

Course summary

This section provides a text summary of the entire course. It is useful for providing closure at the end of the course. The course summary also indicates the next course in this series, if there is one, and lists additional resources you might find useful as you continue to learn about the software.

Quick reference

The quick reference is an at-a-glance job aid summarizing some of the more common features of the software.

Glossary

The glossary provides definitions for all of the key terms used in this course.

Index

The index at the end of this manual makes it easy for you to find information about a particular software component, feature, or concept.

Manual conventions

We've tried to keep the number of elements and the types of formatting to a minimum in the manuals. This aids in clarity and makes the manuals more classically elegant looking. But there are some conventions and icons you should know about.

Convention	Description
Italic text	In conceptual text, indicates a new term or feature.
Bold text	In unit summaries, indicates a key term or concept. In an independent practice activity, indicates an explicit item that you select, choose, or type.
`Code font`	Indicates code or syntax.
`Longer strings of ▶ code will look ▶ like this.`	In the hands-on activities, any code that's too long to fit on a single line is divided into segments by one or more continuation characters (▶). This code should be entered as a continuous string of text.
Select **bold item**	In the left column of hands-on activities, bold sans-serif text indicates an explicit item that you select, choose, or type.
Keycaps like (↵ ENTER)	Indicate a key on the keyboard you must press.

Hands-on activities

The hands-on activities are the most important parts of our manuals. They are divided into two primary columns. The "Here's how" column gives short instructions to you about what to do. The "Here's why" column provides explanations, graphics, and clarifications. Here's a sample:

Do it!

A-1:   Creating a commission formula

Here's how	Here's why
1 Open Sales	This is an oversimplified sales compensation worksheet. It shows sales totals, commissions, and incentives for five sales reps.
2 Observe the contents of cell F4	F4 ▼ **=** =E4*C_Rate The commission rate formulas use the name "C_Rate" instead of a value for the commission rate.

For these activities, we have provided a collection of data files designed to help you learn each skill in a real-world business context. As you work through the activities, you will modify and update these files. Of course, you might make a mistake and, therefore, want to re-key the activity starting from scratch. To make it easy to start over, you will rename each data file at the end of the first activity in which the file is modified. Our convention for renaming files is to add the word "My" to the beginning of the file name. In the above activity, for example, a file called "Sales" is being used for the first time. At the end of this activity, you would save the file as "My sales," thus leaving the "Sales" file unchanged. If you make a mistake, you can start over using the original "Sales" file.

In some activities, however, it may not be practical to rename the data file. If you want to retry one of these activities, ask your instructor for a fresh copy of the original data file.

Introduction   **vii**

Topic B: Setting your expectations

Properly setting your expectations is essential to your success. This topic will help you do that by providing:

- Prerequisites for this course
- A description of the target student at whom the course is aimed
- A list of the objectives for the course
- A skills assessment for the course

Course prerequisites

There are no prerequisites for this course.

Target student

The target student for this course has little or no experience with personal computers. You will get most out of this course if your goal is to learn the basics of personal computers.

Course objectives

These overall course objectives will give you an idea about what to expect from the course. It is also possible that they will help you see that this course is not the right one for you. If you think you either lack the prerequisite knowledge or already know most of the subject matter to be covered, you should let your instructor know that you think you are misplaced in the class.

After completing this course, you will know how to:

- Discuss the evolution of computers, types of PCs, and the Input-Process-Output cycle, and switch on a computer and identify the desktop components.
- Use a keyboard and a mouse and describe other input devices.
- Describe the central processing unit (CPU), random access memory (RAM), and read-only memory (ROM).
- Write-protect and format floppy disks, identify the differences between hard disks and floppy disks, determine the storage capacity of a hard disk, and discuss other storage devices.
- Apply monitor and desktop layout settings and use other output devices such as printers, plotters, and sound cards.
- Use Windows Explorer to browse your hard disk, create folders and files, and protect your computer from viruses.
- Use Windows XP Accessories and Windows Help and Support Center, work with Outlook Express and Internet Explorer 6.0, and shut down a computer.

viii Introduction to Personal Computers

Skills inventory

Use the following form to gauge your skill level entering the class. For each skill listed, rate your familiarity from 1 to 5, with five being the most familiar. *This is not a test.* Rather, it is intended to provide you with an idea of where you're starting from at the beginning of class. If you're wholly unfamiliar with all the skills, you might not be ready for the class. If you think you already understand all of the skills, you might need to move on to the next course in the series. In either case, you should let your instructor know as soon as possible.

Skill	1	2	3	4	5
Identifying types of computers					X
Identifying the hardware components of a computer		X			
Classifying software		X			
Identifying various operating systems	X				
Using a keyboard and a mouse	X			X	
Describing other input devices	X				
Discussing the system unit and the CPU	X				
Describing computer memory	X				
Formatting a floppy disk	X				
Viewing the properties of a hard disk	X				
Discussing other data storage devices	X				
Describing monitors, printers, plotters, and sound cards		X			
Customizing the desktop	X				
Navigating with Windows Explorer	X				
Creating files and folders			X		
Printing, moving, copying, deleting, restoring, and searching files				X	
Using WordPad, Calculator, and Paint		X			
Using the Address Book in Outlook Express	X				
Using Internet Explorer 6.0 to navigate the Web		X			
Accessing Help and shutting down a computer	X		X		

Introduction   **ix**

Topic C: Re-keying the course

If you have the proper hardware and software, you can re-key this course after class. This section explains what you'll need in order to do so, and how to do it.

Computer requirements

To re-key this course, your personal computer must have:

- A keyboard and a mouse
- Pentium 233 MHz processor (or higher)
- At least 128 MB RAM
- At least 1.5 GB available hard disk space
- CD-ROM drive
- 3½ inch floppy disk drive
- 1.44 MB high-density 3½-inch floppy disk
- XGA monitor (800×600 minimum resolution support)
- A printer driver (An actual printer is not required, but you will not be able to complete Unit 6, Topic C unless a driver is installed)
- Internet access, if you want to complete the activities in Unit 7, Topic C and for downloading the latest updates and service packs from www.windowsupdate.com

Setup instructions to re-key the course

Before you re-key the course, you will need to perform the following steps.

1 Install Windows XP Professional on an NTFS partition according to the software manufacturer's instructions. Typical installation of the software is required. Then, install the latest critical updates and service packs from www.windowsupdate.com.

2 If the Getting Started with Windows XP screen appears, clear Show this screen at startup. Click Exit.

3 Adjust the computer's display properties as follows:

   a Right-click anywhere on the desktop to display a shortcut menu.

   b From the shortcut menu, choose Properties to open the Display Properties dialog box.

   c Activate the Themes tab, if necessary.

   d Under Theme, verify Windows XP is selected.

   e Activate the Settings tab.

   f Change the Screen resolution to 1024 by 768 pixels, and the Color quality setting to High (24 bit) or higher.

   g Click OK. If you are prompted to accept the new settings, click OK and click Yes. Then, if necessary, close the Display Properties dialog box.

x   Introduction to Personal Computers

4   Display the My Computer, My Network Places and Internet Explorer icons on the desktop. If they are not there already, use the following steps:

    a   Right-click anywhere on the desktop.

    b   From the shortcut menu, choose Properties.

    c   In the Display Properties dialog box, click the Desktop tab.

    d   Click Customize Desktop to open the Desktop Items dialog box.

    e   Under Desktop icons, check My Computer, My Network Places and Internet Explorer, and clear My Documents.

    f   Click OK to close the Desktop Items dialog box.

    g   Click OK to close the Display Properties dialog box.

5   Display the Quick Launch toolbar on the taskbar by right-clicking the taskbar and choosing Toolbars, Quick Launch.

9   Specify a blank page as the Home Page for Internet Explorer 6.0 as follows (This must be done to key the Unit7, C-1 and C-2 activities properly):

    a   On the desktop, right-click the Internet Explorer icon and choose Properties to open the Internet Properties dialog box with the General tab selected.

    b   Under Home page, click Use Blank.

    c   Click OK.

10   Create an Internet account. You will need Web access in order to complete Unit 7. Consult your Internet service provider (ISP) for details.

12   In Windows Explorer, display the full path in the Address bar and display file extensions as follows:

    a   Right-click Start and then choose Explorer to start Windows Explorer.

    b   In Windows Explorer, choose Tools, Folder Options.

    c   Activate the View tab, if necessary.

    d   Under Advanced settings, check Display the full path in the Address bar, if necessary.

    e   Click OK.

    f   Close Windows Explorer.

9   On each computer, start Outlook Express. The New Connection Wizard starts (sometimes shown as Internet Connection Wizard). A fully functional e-mail account is not necessary for this course. Follow the on-screen prompts in the New Connection Wizard as follows:

    a   Click Cancel. A message box appears to verify that you wish to cancel

    b   Click Yes to close the wizard.

    c   Close Outlook Express.

16   Shut down the machine.

Unit 1

Introduction to computers

Unit time: 50 minutes

Complete this unit, and you'll know how to:

A Discuss the evolution of computers and types of PCs.

B Discuss the Input-Process-Output cycle.

C Switch on a computer, and identify the desktop components.

1–2 Introduction to Personal Computers

Topic A: Overview of computers

Explanation

A *computer* is a machine that you use to store and manipulate information. The earliest computers were as large as a room. But thanks to continuous technological advances over the last 60 years, you can now hold some computers in the palm of your hand. Computers are found in businesses and establishments, such as stores, restaurants, banks, airports, and homes, where they are used to perform a large variety of functions. They are available in a wide range of sizes, shapes, types, and speeds to meet your needs.

Evolution of computers

The first computer was developed in the United States in the 1940s. Since then, technology has progressed with the invention of vacuum tubes, transistors, silicon chips, and microprocessors (CPUs). Today, computers are faster, smaller, more powerful, and more versatile than ever before. Computer technology has advanced to a point where you can connect your computer to a network of computers without even using a cable.

The evolution of computers can be broadly classified as follows:

- **Institutional computing era**. This era was characterized by a few large and expensive computers that were used to meet the data processing requirements of large organizations, government agencies, and scientific and military establishments.

- **Personal computing era**. This era was characterized by small and inexpensive microcomputers (commonly known as *personal computers (PCs)*) that were used by individuals in small organizations, schools, and homes.

- **Interpersonal computing era**. This era is characterized by networks of interconnected computers that organizations, schools, and homes use for communication and data storage and manipulation. This era is also be called the *Internet era* because it's characterized by the development of Internet technology, which has revolutionized the way people work and communicate.

With the progression of computer technology, various types of computers have evolved. They can be classified as follows:

- **Mainframe**: A large and expensive *multi-user* computer on which hundreds of users can work simultaneously on the same data. Mainframes have large data storage capacity and can process bulk data. They are used to perform tasks such as scientific calculations and data processing for large businesses, banks, insurance companies, and manufacturers.

- **Supercomputer**: A very fast computer that can process billions of instructions per second. Supercomputers are used to perform tasks that involve processing large amounts of data, and processing tasks with complex requirements such as weather forecasting, biomedical applications, and aircraft design.

- **Minicomputer**: A multi-user computer that can support 4 to 200 users simultaneously. Minicomputers are used to perform tasks such as hospital administration and manufacturing processes.

- **Personal computer (PC):** A small, single-user computer that you can use to perform a variety of tasks, ranging from maintaining household finances to managing the finances of a large company.
- **Server:** A computer that makes programs and data available to a network of computers. It also handles communication between interconnected computers. Servers can also be used as multi-user computers.

Exhibit 1-1 shows the various types of computers that have evolved over the last few decades.

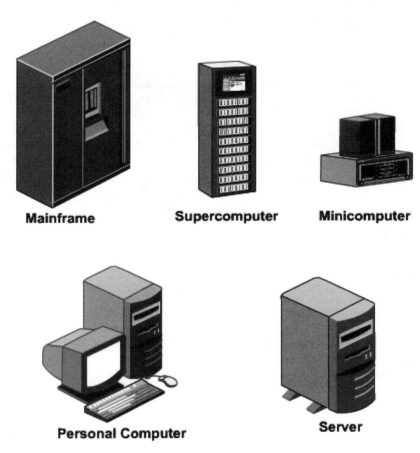

Exhibit 1-1: Types of computers

1–4 Introduction to Personal Computers

Do it!

A-1: Discussing the evolution of computers

Questions and answers

1 What is the difference between the early computers and today's computers?

Size & Cost.

2 If you want to buy a computer for maintaining your household finances, which type of computer would best meet your needs?

PC

3 A large financial organization with 2000 employees wants to buy a computer on which all employees can work simultaneously. Which type of computer should this company buy? *Mainframe*

4 Why are supercomputers used for complex tasks such as weather forecasting?

very fast computer, best for large data

Introduction to computers **1–5**

Benefits and limitations of computers

Explanation

Computers can store, analyze, and retrieve large amounts of information, therefore, they are a popular choice for performing many tasks. Computers also work at very high speeds and rarely make mistakes. Unlike humans, the monotony of repetitive work does not affect computers. For these reasons, the use of computers is spreading to a large number of spheres, ranging from ATM machines to electronic cash registers to multimedia games. However, computers can fail or produce faulty results if the instructions are incorrect or incomplete.

Do it!

A-2: Discussing the benefits and limitations of computers

Questions and answers

1 What are some of the benefits provided by computers?

— Store, analyze – retrieve large amounts of info.
— Fast + accurate calculations.
— monotony does not affect computers (Repetiveness)

2 What will happen if incomplete instructions are provided to a computer?

Incorrect or incomplete instructions lead to faulty Results.

Personal computers

Explanation

The most popular type of computer in use today is the PC. PCs were developed in the early 1980s. Today's PCs are faster and smaller than those sold two decades ago. You can use PCs to perform a diverse range of tasks, for example:

- Writing and editing documents, such as letters, schedules, and reports
- Maintaining large volumes of data
- Managing numbers and performing calculations
- Creating and manipulating graphics
- Using multimedia and playing games
- Representing data in the form of charts and graphs
- Communicating through e-mail and instant messengers
- Buying and selling items by using the Internet
- Learning or researching various subjects and technologies by using the Internet and interactive CD-ROMs

PCs are classified in two categories, desktops and portables. Unlike the earliest computers that occupied a lot of space, desktops can be placed conveniently on a desk (hence, the name). However, desktops are too large and cumbersome to carry while traveling. Portable PCs, on the other hand, can run on batteries, are small in size, and are easy to carry. Exhibit 1-2 shows some of the portable PCs available today.

Exhibit 1-2: Portable PCs

Introduction to computers **1-7**

The following table lists and describes various portable PCs.

PC	Description
Laptop	A portable computer with the same computing power as a desktop, but weighs much less and has a built-in video screen.
Notebook	A computing device with the same processing power as a laptop but is much smaller.
Palmtop	A device that you can hold in the palm of your hand. Palmtops, such as PalmPilots, are among the smallest of all the portables, usually the size of a pocket calculator. You can use palmtops only for limited, built-in applications.
Personal Digital Assistant (PDA)	A handheld device originally designed as a personal organizer. It includes a clock, a date book, an address book, a task list, a memo pad, and a simple calculator.
Tablet PC	A computer that looks like a notebook. It has a screen on which a user can write with a special purpose pen.
Wearable computer	A small personal computer that users can wear while operating. This device is being developed and designed to act as an intelligent assistant.

Do it!

A-3:   Discussing types of PCs

Questions and answers

1 What are the two types of PCs?

Desktops & portable

2 How was the name "desktop" derived?

3 Which computers would you categorize as portables?

4 What does the term "palm" in palmtops and PalmPilots indicate?

Topic B: How computers work

Explanation

Computers operate according to the *Input-Process-Output* (*I-P-O*) principle that characterizes most production processes. Computers accept the data you enter as input, process it, and then produce information as output. A computer's physical components, called *hardware*, are used during all three phases of the I-P-O cycle. To use the various hardware components in the I-P-O cycle, computers require sets of instructions called *software*.

The Input-Process-Output cycle

Most activities follow the I-P-O cycle. For example, to manufacture an automobile, the input is the raw material, such as the body mold, engine parts, and wheels. The process involves building the automobile. It uses the input to produce the output—in this case, an automobile.

A computer also follows the I-P-O cycle. By entering data and instructions by using a keyboard or other input device, such as a mouse or scanner, you supply input to the computer. A component of the computer system, the *microprocessor* or *CPU* (Central Processing Unit), processes the input and creates the information known as the output. The output most frequently appears on the computer screen or can be produced in print by using a computer printer. Exhibit 1-3 shows the I-P-O cycle for a computer.

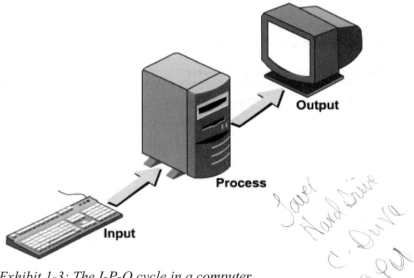

Exhibit 1-3: The I-P-O cycle in a computer

Introduction to computers   **1–9**

Do it!   **B-1:   Discussing the Input-Process-Output cycle**

Questions and answers

1 Describe the I-P-O cycle as it pertains to computers.

Input
process
  output

2 Which component of a computer does the processing?

3 While using a computer to calculate the sum of two numbers, what would you characterize as the input, process, and output?

1–10   Introduction to Personal Computers

Hardware

Explanation

Computer hardware is required for all three phases of the I-P-O cycle. In addition to the keyboard and the mouse, you can use other input devices such as trackballs, joysticks, scanners, pen-input or digitizing tablets, touch pads, and digital cameras. The most common output devices are monitors and printers.

The following table lists and describes the basic hardware components.

Device	Description
System unit	A box that contains various electronic components and circuitry required to run a computer
Microprocessor (CPU)	A component inside the system unit that processes input and generates output
Monitor	A video screen that displays the user interface of the active software program(s)
Keyboard	An input device used for entering letters, numbers, and other characters; you can also use the keyboard to navigate menus and run commands
Mouse	An input device used for pointing to and selecting options; moving the mouse moves an arrow-head pointer on the monitor
Printer	(Optional) An output device used for transferring output to paper

Most computers also have the ability to play sounds, or music, and connect to the Internet. Speakers and headphones are output devices that allow you to listen to sounds on your computer. To use speakers or headphones, however, your computer must have an additional processing component called a *sound card.*

A *modem* (*modulator demodulator*) is a communication device that allows you to access the Internet. To use a modem, you need communication software that allows your computer to interact with the device.

Do it!

B-2: Discussing hardware

Questions and answers

1 List some examples of input devices other than the mouse and the keyboard.

2 Which device do banks use for issuing account statements to customers?

3 Which hardware components allow you to listen to music on your computer?

4 Which hardware component is required to access the Internet?

Software

Explanation

Software is a set of instructions that a computer requires to perform various tasks, such as managing hardware components, creating a document, and sending e-mail messages. There are two categories of software, system and application. Each category handles a different type of computer instruction.

System software

System software controls hardware components such as the mouse, the keyboard, and the computer's memory. It also ensures that the instructions received from a user are correctly interpreted. System software consists of an operating system and basic utility software, such as device controller software.

Application software

Application software is designed for specific purposes such as creating documents, browsing the Internet, and accounting. There is a wide variety of application software available to help you perform these and many more tasks. For example, you can create and manage documents by using word processing software, maintain household expenses by using spreadsheet software, and write to friends by using e-mail software. Exhibit 1-4 shows some examples of application software.

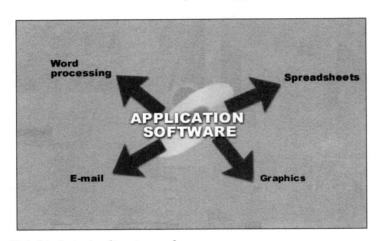

Exhibit 1-4: Application software

Do it!

B-3: Discussing software

Questions and answers

1 What are the two categories of software?

System software
application ware.

2 Which type of software coordinates the functions of hardware components?

System Software

3 When you print a letter, which type of software manages the printer?

application Software

4 What are some types of application software used in day-to-day activities?

Exam. *microsoft word*
ITunes-

iPOD- Hardware

1-14 Introduction to Personal Computers

Operating systems

Explanation

An *operating system* (OS) is software that carries out the basic functions of a computer. These functions include recognizing input from the keyboard, sending output to the monitor, and keeping track of files. The operating system provides an environment for hardware and software to work together. Operating systems such as UNIX, Linux, Macintosh, Windows 98, Windows 2000, Windows 2003, Windows XP, and Windows Me are part of the system software. An operating system might have all or some of the following characteristics:

- Multitasking: Simultaneously running multiple programs
- Multiprocessing: Running a program on multiple microprocessors (CPUs), leading to an increase in the processing speed
- Multi-user: Simultaneously running the same program for multiple users
- Built-in support for graphics
- Built-in support for networks

An operating system can be one of two types, single user and multi-user. A single-user operating system, such as Windows 98 or Windows 2000, provides access to one user at a time. It's typically used in offices, homes, and computer labs in educational institutions.

A multi-user operating system, such as Windows 2000 Server, Windows Server 2003, UNIX, or Linux, provides access to multiple users at the same time. It's typically used when several users need to work simultaneously on the same data.

Do it!

B-4: Discussing types of operating systems

Questions and answers
1 What is an operating system?
2 Name a few single-user operating systems.
3 Name a few multi-user operating systems.

Introduction to computers **1–15**

Topic C: Starting a computer

Explanation

Your computer must have an operating system installed before it can perform any task. Before you switch on a computer, you must ensure that all the cables are connected to the appropriate sockets (referring to the manual is recommended). When you switch on the system unit, the operating system automatically begins a process known as *booting*, which starts the computer. Next, you switch on the monitor and any other attached devices such as a printer, a scanner, or speakers.

Desktop components

After you switch on the computer, the operating system (Windows XP for this course) displays a desktop, as shown in Exhibit 1-5. Just as a physical desktop contains the tools that you use to work, the Windows XP desktop contains programs (also called applications) that you use to perform tasks such as creating and editing documents, working with storage devices, and printing documents.

The Windows XP desktop contains icons and a taskbar. *Icons* are pictorial representations of the programs included in Windows XP. You click an icon to start the application associated with it. The *taskbar* is located at the bottom of the screen. It contains the *Start* button, the *Quick Launch toolbar*, and the *notification area*. The following table describes these components.

Component	Description
Start button	Used to start applications, get help, configure the computer, and shut down your computer
Quick Launch toolbar	Used to display the desktop, launch Internet Explorer (an application used to access the Internet), or launch Windows Media Player (an application used to play digital media)
Notification area	Contains a clock and displays the status of specific programs and controls

1–16 Introduction to Personal Computers

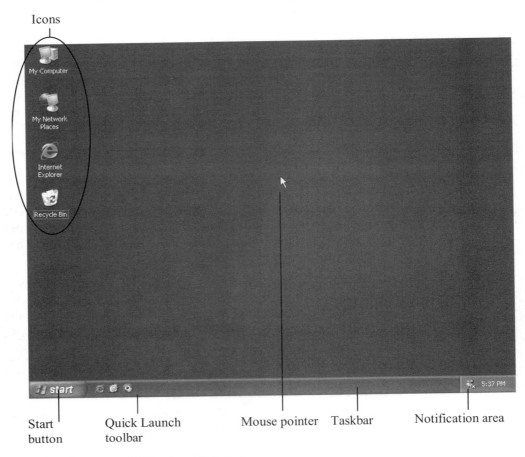

Exhibit 1-5: A sample Windows XP desktop

Do it!

Introduction to computers   **1–17**

C-1: Identifying the desktop components

Here's how	Here's why
1 Follow your instructor's directions to switch on your computer	
2 Log on to Windows XP	(If necessary.) Follow your instructor's directions.
Click **OK**	The Windows XP desktop appears.
3 Observe the desktop	(A sample desktop is shown in Exhibit 1-5.) It contains icons of some commonly used Windows XP programs and a taskbar.
4 Observe the icons	You use icons to quickly start their associated applications.
5 Observe the taskbar	(At the bottom of the screen.) You use it to navigate within Windows XP. It contains the Start button, the Quick Launch toolbar, and the notification area.
Observe the Start button	(On the taskbar.) You can use this button to start applications, get help, and set up (configure) and turn off your computer.
Observe the Quick Launch toolbar	(On the taskbar.) You click the icons on this toolbar to launch Internet Explorer (an application used to access the Internet), display the desktop, or run Windows Media Player (an application used to play digital media).
Observe the notification area	(In the lower-right corner of the screen on the taskbar.) It contains a clock that displays the time.
Observe the arrow on the desktop	This arrow is referred to as the mouse pointer or simply, the pointer. You use it for various activities such as selecting an icon on the desktop or starting an application.
6 Point to the clock	(On the notification area.) A message, called a ScreenTip, appears showing the current weekday and date.

Unit summary: Introduction to computers

Topic A
In this topic, you learned about the **evolution** of computers. You also learned that the types of computers available today include **personal computers (PCs)**, **servers**, **minicomputers**, **mainframes**, and **supercomputers**. Then, you learned about the benefits and limitations of computers. Finally, you learned about the uses of PCs and about **desktops** and **portables**.

Topic B
In this topic, you learned about the **Input-Process-Output** cycle that a computer uses to process data. You learned that **hardware** refers to the computer's physical components and that **software** is a set of instructions to use these physical components. You also learned about types of **operating systems**.

Topic C
In this topic, you learned about switching on a computer and the activities associated with it. You also identified the Windows XP **desktop components**, which include **icons**, the **taskbar**, the **Start button**, the **Quick Launch toolbar**, and the **notification area**.

Review questions

1 Joe wants to buy a computer for maintaining accounts at his department store. Which type of computer do you think he should buy?

2 Which types of computers allow multiple users to work simultaneously?

3 List three tasks that you might perform with the help of a computer.

4 Sally wants to buy a PC that she can use at home and at the office. Which type of PC would you suggest to her?

5 Jane works in the Human Resources department at her company. She needs to retrieve personnel details about an employee from the company database. She can find this information by using the employee's social security number. Identify the input, process, and output elements involved in this transaction.

6 An airline reservation system is an example of which type of software?

1–20 Introduction to Personal Computers

Unit 2

Input devices

Unit time: 30 minutes

Complete this unit, and you'll know how to:

A Use a mouse and a keyboard.

B Describe other input devices.

2–2   Introduction to Personal Computers

Topic A: Mouse and keyboard basics

Explanation

You use input devices to enter data and provide instructions to a computer. The most common input devices are the mouse and the keyboard.

Mouse

The *mouse* is an input device you can use to select items and launch programs. A mouse usually has two or three buttons, although mouse devices with four or more buttons have also been created. In addition to buttons, a mouse can have a wheel button that you use to scroll through documents. By default, the left mouse button is the *primary mouse button*. However, you can designate the right mouse button as the primary mouse button if required.

As you move the mouse, a pointing arrow, called the *mouse pointer*, moves on the screen. You can perform the following types of operations with the mouse:

- **Pointing**: Positioning the mouse pointer over an object.
- **Clicking**: Pressing and releasing the left mouse button.
- **Double-clicking**: Pressing and releasing the left mouse button twice in rapid succession.
- **Dragging**: Holding down the left mouse button while moving the mouse pointer. This activity is also referred to as *drag and drop*.
- **Right-clicking**: Pressing and releasing the right mouse button.

You use the left mouse button to select, move, and open objects. You use the right mouse button to display an object's shortcut menu, which contains the frequently used commands associated with that object.

Do it!

A-1:   Using the mouse

Here's how	Here's why
1 Point to the **My Computer** icon as indicated	
	A ScreenTip appears, describing the function of the icon.
Click the mouse button	The icon changes color, indicating that it's selected.
2 Press and hold the mouse button	On the My Computer icon.
Move the pointer to another location on the desktop	(Continue holding the mouse button while you're moving the pointer.) This process is called dragging.
Release the mouse button	The My Computer icon appears in a new location.
3 Drag the **My Computer** icon back to its original location	

Input devices **2–3**

4	Click **Start**	
		To display the Start menu. The section of the Start menu shown here contains the programs you select most often. This list is updated automatically as you run different programs. Your menu items might differ from those shown here.
5	Observe the All Programs command and the right-facing arrow next to it	The arrow indicates that this command contains submenus.
6	Point to **All Programs**	To display the All Programs submenu.
7	Point to **Accessories**	To display the Accessories submenu.
8	Choose **WordPad**	(Point to it and click.) To start WordPad. The application window appears on the desktop.
	Observe the taskbar	A button appears on the taskbar when you start an application.
9	Point to the taskbar button and right-click	
		To display a shortcut menu for the taskbar button.
10	Choose **Close**	To close WordPad.

Keyboard

Explanation

You use a keyboard to enter alphanumeric characters. You can also use a keyboard to navigate menus, execute commands, and enter other program instructions. A flashing vertical line (called an *insertion point*) on the screen indicates the position where you can start typing the characters. When you press a character key, the corresponding character appears at the insertion point, and the insertion point moves one position forward.

Exhibit 2-1 shows a keyboard with some commonly used keys labeled.

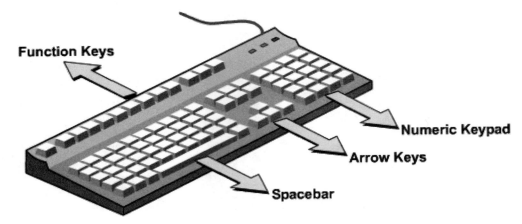

Exhibit 2-1: A keyboard

Input devices   **2–5**

The following table describes some of the commonly used keys and their functions.

Key	Description
↵ ENTER or RETURN	Executes an instruction or begins a new paragraph.
CAPS LOCK	If on, the letters that you type appear in uppercase. Otherwise, they appear in lowercase.
NUM LOCK	Activates the numeric keys on the numeric keypad, located on the right side of the keyboard.
SHIFT	If Caps Lock is off, pressing a character key while holding Shift inserts the character in uppercase. If Caps Lock is on, pressing the character key while holding Shift inserts the character in lowercase. Pressing a key with two symbols while holding Shift inserts the upper symbol.
CTRL, ALT	(Control key and Alt key, respectively; Alt is an abbreviation for Alternative yet the key is commonly referred to as "Alt key") These keys execute a command when pressed in combination with other keys. For example, in most application software, pressing the character "F" while holding Alt (Alt+F) conveniently displays the File menu. You can use the File menu to perform tasks such as opening a new file, saving and closing a file, and closing an application.
SPACEBAR	Inserts a blank space at the position of the insertion point.
← BACKSPACE	Deletes the character to the left of the insertion point.
↑, ↓, ←, →	(Arrow keys) Move the insertion point in the direction indicated on the key.
HOME	Moves the insertion point to the beginning of a line.
END	Moves the insertion point to the end of a line.
PAGE UP	Moves the insertion point one page up. The visible screen area in an application is one page.
PAGE DOWN	Moves the insertion point one page down.
INSERT	If you press a character key when it's on, the character appears at the insertion point. If off, the character that you press replaces the character to the right of the insertion point.
DELETE	Deletes the character to the right of the insertion point.
ESC	(Escape key) Usually used for canceling a command. Its function depends on the application.
F1 – F12	(Function keys) Perform special functions, such as printing a document or displaying help, depending on the software you're using.

2–6   Introduction to Personal Computers

Do it!   ## A-2: Using the keyboard

Here's how	Here's why
1 Start WordPad	Click Start, and then choose All Programs, Accessories, WordPad.
2 Observe the flashing vertical line	This line is the insertion point. It indicates where text will appear when you start typing.
Type your full name in lowercase letters	(Don't use the Shift key.) Press the Spacebar as needed to insert spaces.
3 Press (HOME)	To move the insertion point to the beginning of the line.
4 Press (DELETE)	To delete the first letter of your name. You can press the Delete key again to delete another letter.
5 While holding (SHIFT), type the first letter of your name	The first letter of your name now appears in uppercase.
Release (SHIFT)	
Press (END)	To move the insertion point to the end of the line.
6 Use the left arrow key to position the insertion point at the beginning of your last name	
Press (DELETE)	To delete the first letter of your last name.
Type the first letter of your last name in uppercase	Use Shift.
7 Choose **File**, **Exit**	(From the WordPad menu.) To close WordPad. A message box appears asking you to confirm whether you want to save changes to the document.
Click **No**	To close WordPad without saving the document.

Input devices **2–7**

Topic B: Other input devices

Explanation

In addition to the mouse and the keyboard, advances in technology have led to the development of several types of input devices, which make it easier for you to input information into a computer. These input devices include a mouse with a wheel button, light pens, touch screens, trackballs, joysticks, scanners, pen input/digitizing tablets, touch pads, digital cameras, Optical Character Recognition devices, Optical Mark Reader devices, and microphones. Exhibit 2-2 shows some of these devices.

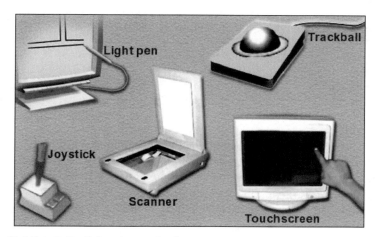

Exhibit 2-2: Other input devices

The following table describes different types of input devices.

Device	Description
Mouse with a wheel button	You rotate the wheel button to scroll up and down in an application. This type of mouse is available with two, three, or five buttons. You can customize these buttons.
Light pen	A device similar to a pen that you use to select an option on the screen by pointing to it. You can also use a light pen to draw an image by sketching it directly on the monitor. Light pens are useful for drawing objects in Computer Aided Designing (CAD), where you use the pen to select colors and line thickness, reduce or enlarge drawings, and edit drawings.
Touch screen	A monitor that makes it easier for you to select an option by pointing to it with your finger. Touch screens are used in information kiosks such as those found in conference and exhibition centers, grocery, drug, and department stores, travel agencies, and museums. Some ATM machines also have touch screens, which you use to deposit and withdraw cash.
Trackball	A pointing device with a ball resting within a case (similar to an inverted mouse). Trackballs are used with portable computers. Trackball Explorer and Trackball Optical are examples of trackballs.

Device	Description
Joystick	A lever that can move in all directions, controlling a pointer or some other symbol on a monitor. This device is commonly used to play video or multimedia games.
Scanners	A device that you use to copy an existing image (referred to as *scanning*) and store it on your computer. You can then modify these images.
Pen input/digitizing tablets	A set consisting of an electronic pen and an electromagnetic tablet that you can use as high-tech drawing tools. These tools are suitable for drawing high-quality sketches, tracing intricate patterns, and performing photo restoration.
Touch pad	A stand-alone pointing device on which you tap gently to move around on the desktop. These devices reduce the stress on fingers.
Digital camera	A camera that you use to take photographs that can be transferred to a computer without scanning them.
Optical Character Recognition (OCR)	A device that you use to recognize each character in a photographic image of printed or handwritten text. This device is commonly used to read bar codes or sort letters at post offices by reading postal codes.
Optical Mark Reader (OMR)	A device that scans pencil marks by using infrared light. This device is commonly used to scan answer sheets for multiple-choice questions or lottery tickets.
Microphone	A device that converts sound into electrical signals. This device is commonly used for two-way audio communication on the Internet.

Do it!

Input devices   **2–9**

B-1:   Discussing other input devices

Question and answers

1   List the input devices that function similar to the mouse.

2   A graphic artist wants to use an input device that simplifies creating graphics. Which input device should the graphic artist use?

3   If John wants to store a photograph of his son on a computer, which device should he use?

4   Robert wants to restore a torn photograph. Which device should he use?

5   The constant use of the mouse strains Joan's fingers. Which device can she use instead to relieve the stress on her fingers?

6   Peter wants to process a large number of multiple-choice questions marked with pencil. Which device should he use?

2-10 Introduction to Personal Computers

Unit summary: Input devices

Topic A   In this topic, you learned how to use the most common input devices, the **mouse** and the **keyboard**. You learned about the types of actions that you can perform by using the mouse buttons. You also identified the keys on the keyboard.

Topic B   In this topic, you learned about other input devices such as **a mouse with a wheel button**, **light pens**, **touch screens**, **trackballs**, **joysticks**, **scanners**, **pen input/digitizing tablets**, **touch pads**, **digital cameras**, **Optical Character Recognition**, **Optical Mark Reader**, and **microphones**.

Independent practice activity

1   On the desktop, drag the Internet Explorer icon to another location.

2   Drag the icon back to its original location.

3   Start Notepad. (From the Start menu, choose All Programs, Accessories, Notepad.)

4   Press the key that will make the letters you type appear in uppercase.

5   Type your last name in uppercase letters.

6   Move to the beginning of the line.

7   Type your first name in lowercase letters.

8   Leave a blank space between your first name and last name.

9   Move to the end of the line.

10 Close Notepad without saving the file.

Review questions

1   Which mouse action requires you to hold down the mouse button while moving the mouse on the mouse pad?

2   On the keyboard, which keys can be used to perform special functions, such as printing a document or displaying help, depending on the software you're using?

3   Which of the following input devices move around in parallel on the desktop with the mouse pointer on screen?

   A   Mouse

   B   Touch pad

   C   Joystick

   D   Mouse with a wheel button

Input devices   **2–11**

4 Which keys must be used in combination with other keys to execute a command?

5 What is the difference between OCR and OMR?

2–12   Introduction to Personal Computers

Unit 3

Processing data

Unit time: 30 minutes

Complete this unit, and you'll know how to:

A Identify the components of the system unit and the CPU and discuss their functions.

B Describe the types of computer memory, RAM and ROM.

Topic A: The system unit and the CPU

Explanation

The *central processing unit (CPU)* is a set of electronic components that interprets the data you enter, processes it, and generates the output. The components of the CPU are housed on a common platform called the *motherboard*. The motherboard, along with other components, is in turn housed in the system unit.

System unit components

Although the CPU is the central component of a computer, there are many other components that comprise the system unit. Each component of the system unit performs a different task. Some of the components are shown in Exhibit 3-1.

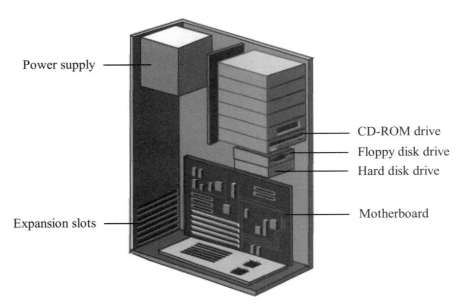

Exhibit 3-1: The components of a system unit

The following table lists and describes the components of a system unit.

Component	Function
Motherboard	A large board inside the system unit that houses the CPU and other components. All the input/output devices are connected to the motherboard.
CPU	The CPU processes the input to the computer. The term CPU is often used interchangeably with microprocessor. One of the ways to quantify microprocessors is their speed of processing instructions. The units for measuring the speed of a microprocessor are megahertz (MHz) and gigahertz (GHz). One megahertz means 1 million cycles per second and 1gigahertz means 1 billion cycles per second. As a comparison, a 200 GHz microprocessor is faster than a 200 MHz microprocessor, and a 300 GHz microprocessor is faster than a 200 GHz microprocessor.
Memory	Tiny electronic circuits that store data for processing. It is the internal memory of a computer present on the motherboard.

Component	Function
Hard disk drive	Reads data from and writes data to the hard disk. The hard disk is a storage device where the computer stores large amounts of data and instructions.
Floppy disk drive	Reads data from and writes data to a floppy disk. Floppy disks can be used to store small amounts of information. They are removable and suitable for transferring data from one computer to another.
CD-ROM drive	Reads information from CD-ROMs. CD-ROMs are removable storage devices that store much more information than floppy disks.
Power supply	Supplies voltage to the internal components and external devices. The power switch of the system unit is a part of the power supply unit.
Fan	Cools the power supply.
Speaker	Produces sound.
Expansion slots	A set of sockets that you use to attach additional input and output devices to your computer. You can also use these slots to add more memory.
Ports	An interface to which you connect a device. There are three types of ports: serial, parallel, and USB. Serial and parallel ports are generally used to connect devices such as a keyboard, a mouse, a printer, and a modem. However, USB ports are replacing serial and parallel ports because you can connect external devices through USB ports without restarting a computer. There is another type of port called an infrared port. It allows two computers or a computer and a device to communicate without the use of wires.

Do it!

A-1: Identifying the components of a system unit

Questions and answers

1 Which component of the motherboard does the actual processing of data?

2 What are the units of measurement for the speed of a microprocessor?

3 Which component of the system unit stores data for processing?

4 Which removable storage device can store large amounts of information?

Central processing unit

Explanation

The CPU performs a variety of input operations, such as arithmetic operations and comparison operations. Arithmetic operations include addition, subtraction, multiplication, and division. Comparison operations include checking to see if two quantities are equal or if one quantity is larger than another. Performing arithmetic and comparison operations quickly is commonly known as *number crunching*. In addition to its number crunching operations, the CPU responds to requests from peripheral devices, such as printers and scanners, as shown in Exhibit 3-2. As the name central processing unit implies, the CPU is responsible for carrying out virtually all computer operations.

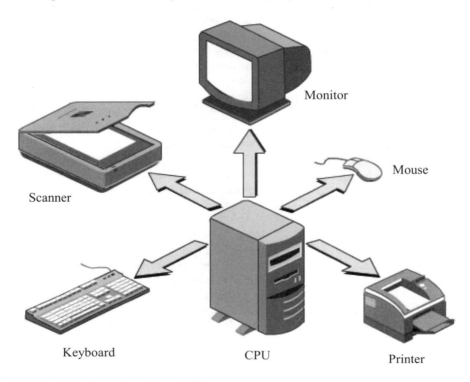

Exhibit 3-2: The role of the CPU

In the CPU, the task of executing a computer operation is divided between the *control unit*, which directs the flow of instructions to be executed and the *arithmetic-logic unit (ALU)*, which executes the computer operation.

Do it!

A-2: Discussing the CPU

Questions and answers

1 What are the functions of the CPU?

2 John has used the print command to print a document. Which part of the computer ensures that the print command is carried out?

3 When you enter two numbers to be added as input, which part of the CPU performs the addition?

3-6 Introduction to Personal Computers

Topic B: Memory

Explanation

Memory stores the data and instructions that the CPU processes as well as the output of the processed data. Memory is a collection of storage cells, each of which can store one *binary digit* (*bit*), which is the smallest unit of information for a computer. The value of a bit can be 1 or 0. Memory is measured in terms of *bytes*. A byte is a group of eight bits. Therefore, a byte is a series of eight 1s and 0s arranged in various sequences that can be interpreted by the computer. The amount of memory a computer has is measured in kilobytes, megabytes, and gigabytes. The following table lists the equivalent values of each of these units of measurement.

Unit	Equivalent
Byte	8 bits
Kilobyte (KB)	1024 bytes
Megabyte (MB)	1024 KB
Gigabyte (GB)	1024 MB

Memory can be classified as random access memory (RAM) and read-only memory (ROM).

Random access memory (RAM)

RAM is the memory that stores data and instructions temporarily; that is, while the computer is switched on. The data and instructions that are to be used are moved from the hard disk to the memory in a process called *loading*. It's much faster for the microprocessor to go to and from RAM for data and instructions than to go to and from the hard disk. This is because RAM exists in computer chips, which use a technology that is much faster to write data to and read data from than the technology employed in hard disks. However, because RAM is temporary storage, the data and instructions stored in it are lost when you switch off your computer. In contrast, the data and instructions stored on the hard disk are retained even when the computer is switched off.

The speed of a computer depends on the storage capacity of its RAM. The larger the number of bytes that the RAM can store, the faster the computer can perform tasks.

Processing data **3–7**

Do it!

B-1: Describing random access memory

Questions and answers

1 Why are data and instructions copied to RAM before being processed?

2 What is the process of copying data and instructions to RAM called?

3 How many bytes are in one kilobyte?

4 The configuration of Sandra's computer is the same as that of your computer. However, Sandra's computer has 128 MB RAM and your computer has 64 MB RAM. Whose computer will be faster? Why?

Read-only memory (ROM)

Explanation

ROM is memory that can be read but not changed. It is sometimes referred to as nonvolatile storage because its contents remain in storage even when the power is switched off. ROM chips are used for storage of the computer's essential software, called *firmware*. For example, when you switch on a computer, it is the firmware that initiates the booting process.

Do it!

B-2: Describing read-only memory

Questions and answers

1 What are the differences between RAM and ROM?

2 Why is ROM said to be a permanent storage area?

Unit summary: Processing data

Topic A
In this topic, you learned about the components of a **system unit**. You also learned that the **central processing unit (CPU)** processes data and performs tasks in response to the requests of peripheral devices, such as a keyboard.

Topic B
In this topic, you learned that internal memory is classified as **random access memory (RAM)** and **read-only memory (ROM)**. You also learned that RAM is temporary memory that stores data and instructions required by the microprocessor to perform tasks. Finally, you learned that ROM stores **firmware** permanently.

Review questions

1 Which part of a computer responds to requests from peripheral devices?

2 Where in the system unit is the CPU located?

3 Which component of the CPU reads data and instructions stored on a floppy disk?

4 How many bits make up one byte?

5 What happens to the contents of RAM when you switch off a computer?

6 Which components affect a computer's performance the most?

7 Which type of memory (RAM or ROM) can you write to?

Unit 4
Data storage

Unit time: 45 minutes

Complete this unit, and you'll know how to:

A Write-protect and format floppy disks.

B Identify the differences between hard disks and floppy disks, and determine the storage capacity of a hard disk.

C Discuss other storage devices.

Topic A: Floppy disks

Explanation

Data and instructions are stored on devices, such as floppy disks, hard disks, and CD-ROMs. These devices vary in their storage capacity and speed of storing and retrieving data. A floppy disk stores only a small amount of data, typically 1.44 MB. The floppy disk drive, which is a component of the system unit, stores and retrieves data from a floppy disk. Because floppy disks are portable, they provide a convenient means of transferring relatively small amounts of data from one computer to another.

Write-protecting floppy disks

You can read from as well as write to a floppy disk. Therefore, it's possible to overwrite data by mistake. To prevent files from being deleted or changed, you can *write-protect* the disk. To write protect a floppy disk, slide the write-protect tab on the disk to the open position, as shown in Exhibit 4-1.

Exhibit 4-1: A floppy disk

Do it!

A-1: Write-protecting a floppy disk

Here's how	Here's why
1 Follow the instructor's directions on how to hold the floppy disk	
2 Slide the write-protect tab to the open position	To write-protect the floppy disk. This indicates that now you cannot write to the floppy disk.
3 Slide the tab back	To disable write-protection. You can now write to the floppy disk.

Data storage **4–3**

Formatting floppy disks

Explanation

The storage area on a floppy disk is divided into a series of concentric circles called *tracks*. These tracks are further divided into *sectors*, as shown in Exhibit 4-2. Tracks and sectors are numbered, which makes it easier to write and locate data stored on a disk. The number of tracks and sectors determines the *storage capacity* of a disk, which is the amount of information it can store.

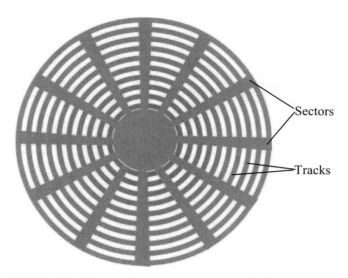

Exhibit 4-2: The tracks and sectors on a disk

Formatting a floppy disk is the process of checking the disk for bad sectors and then allocating tracks and sectors on the recording area. Floppy disks that have not been formatted are unusable. Most floppy disks available on the market are preformatted. However, if you buy unformatted floppy disks, the first thing you need to do is format them. It is a good idea to format a disk if you want to reuse it.

4-4 Introduction to Personal Computers

Do it!

A-2: Formatting a floppy disk

Here's how	Here's why
1 Follow your instructor's directions to insert the floppy disk in the floppy disk drive	
2 Double-click **My Computer**	(Click the My Computer icon twice in rapid succession.) To open the My Computer window.
3 Under Devices with Removable Storage, right-click **3 1/2 Floppy (A:)**	**Open** Explore Search… Sharing and Security… Copy Disk… Format… Cut Copy Create Shortcut Rename Properties To display the shortcut menu. The menu on your computer might not be identical to the one shown here.
Choose **Format…**	To open the Format 3 1/2 Floppy (A:) dialog box. A dialog box is an interactive window in Windows XP applications where you specify any required information.
4 Observe the disk's capacity	Capacity: 3.5", 1.44MB, 512 bytes/sector
5 Under Format options, check **Quick Format**	Format options ☑ Quick Format ☐ Enable Compression ☐ Create an MS-DOS startup disk Quick Format is used to format the disk without checking it for bad sectors.

Data storage   **4–5**

6	Click in the Volume label box	**Volume label**
		To place the insertion point in the box.
	Enter **MyFloppy**	The text in the Volume label box identifies your floppy disk.
7	Click **Start**	A message box appears, warning that formatting will erase all the data on the disk.
	Click **OK**	To begin formatting. A message box appears when the formatting completes.
8	Click **OK**	To close the message box.
9	Click **Close**	To close the Format 3 1/2 Floppy (A:) dialog box.
10	Choose **File**, **Close**	To close the My Computer window.

Topic B: Hard disks

Explanation

A *hard disk* is a storage device inside the system unit that's used to store large amounts of data. You can check the total storage capacity of a hard disk and the amount of remaining space available for storing additional data on the disk.

A hard disk is the main device that a computer uses to store information. It's housed in a self-contained box called the hard disk drive. A personal computer might contain up to eight disks, called *platters*, each of which is divided into tracks and sectors, as shown in Exhibit 4-3. Data is transferred magnetically to and from the hard disk by a read/write head installed within the hard disk drive.

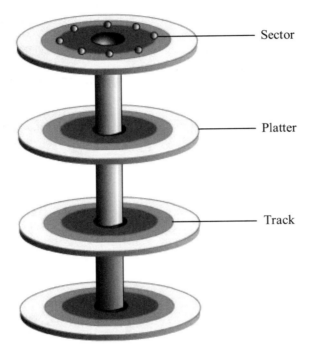

Exhibit 4-3: The platters in a hard disk

Hard disks offer many advantages over floppy disks. Hard disks are installed inside the system unit so they are less prone to damage than floppy disks. Hard disks can store larger quantities of data. Also, a computer can write to and read from a hard disk much faster than from floppy disks.

Do it!

B-1: Discussing hard disks

Questions and answers

1 Which of the storage devices, floppy disk or hard disk, can be read from and written to faster?

2 Which storage device, floppy disk or hard disk, would you use to store large amounts of data?

3 Data is transferred magnetically to and from a hard disk by what component?

Hard disk capacity

Explanation

You can view the properties of a hard disk to determine the disk's total capacity, the used space, and the free space. To view the properties of a hard disk, double-click the My Computer icon on the desktop, right-click Local Disk (C:), and choose Properties to open the Properties dialog box, as shown in Exhibit 4-4. Today, hard disks generally have a capacity between 30GB and 800GB.

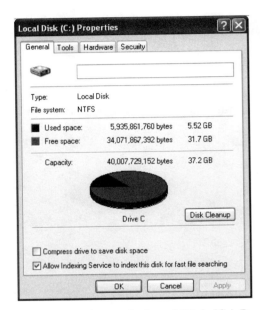

Exhibit 4-4: A sample Local Disk (C:) Properties dialog box

Do it!

Data storage   **4–9**

B-2: Checking the capacity of a hard disk

Here's how	Here's why
1 Open the My Computer window	On the desktop, double-click My Computer.
Observe the icon for the hard disk drive	Local Disk (C:)
	In Windows XP, the hard drive is referred to as the Local Disk (C:) drive by default.
2 Right-click **Local Disk (C:)**	**Open** Explore Search... Sharing and Security... Format... Copy Create Shortcut Rename Properties
	To display the shortcut menu containing commonly used commands for the hard drive. Your menu might not be identical to the one shown here.
Choose **Properties**	To open the Local Disk (C:) Properties dialog box.
3 Observe the Local Disk (C:) Properties dialog box	It shows the capacity of the hard disk, the used space, and the free space (an example is shown in Exhibit 4-4). Your dialog box might not be identical to the one shown in the exhibit.
4 Click **OK**	To close the dialog box.
5 Close the My Computer window	Choose File, Close.

Topic C: Other storage devices

Explanation

In addition to floppy disks and hard disks, you can store data on a variety of other media, such as CD-ROMs, DVDs, Click disks, keydrives, SuperDisks, Zip disks, Optical disks, Magnetic strips, Smart cards, portable hard drives, and rewritable CDs.

CD-ROMs

A *CD-ROM* (*Compact Disc Read-Only Memory*), as shown in Exhibit 4-5, is a removable storage device that can store a large amount of information. You store information on it by using a *CD-Recorder* and retrieve information by running the CD-ROM on a CD-ROM drive.

Exhibit 4-5: A CD-ROM in a CD-ROM tray

CD-ROMs are widely used for storing software that you can install on your computer by copying it to your hard disk. They are also used to store multimedia games, music, movies, and references such as encyclopedias and dictionaries.

DVDs

DVDs (*Digital Video Devices*) store the same type of information as CD-ROMs. However, DVDs can store much more data than CD-ROMs. In addition, the sound and video quality of DVDs is much better. Data stored on a DVD cannot be accessed by using a CD-ROM drive; DVDs require a DVD drive. However, data stored on a CD-ROM can be accessed by using a DVD drive. To write to or manipulate the data stored on a DVD, you use a *DVD recorder*.

Do it!

C-1: Discussing CD-ROMs and DVDs

Questions and answers

1 Which device would you use to store information on a CD-ROM?

2 Why is most commercial software distributed on CD-ROMs rather than on floppy disks?

3 If you want to watch your favorite movie, which would you prefer, a CD-ROM or a DVD? Why?

Other removable storage devices

Explanation

You can use many other removable storage devices in addition to floppy disks, CD-ROMs, and DVDs. These devices include Click disks, keydrives, SuperDisks, Zip disks, Optical disks, Magnetic strips, Smart cards, portable hard drives, and rewritable CDs. Some of these devices are shown in Exhibit 4-6.

Exhibit 4-6: Other removable storage devices

The following table lists the storage capacity and uses for other removable storage devices.

Device	Capacity	Used for...
Click disk	40 MB	Digital cameras or notebook computers
Keydrive (USB flash drive)	32 MB to 512 MB	Transferring large amounts of data, for example, between home and office. Ideal for use in laptops; similar in size to a small key ring
SuperDisk	150 MB	Transferring large amounts of data between computers
Zip disk	100 MB and 250 MB	Transferring large amounts of data between computers
Optical disk	100 MB	Storing large picture files and photographs in a digital camera
Magnetic strip		Storing small amounts of information such as the personal identity number on a credit card
Smart card	1KB to 32 KB	Storing information such as phone numbers and phone settings, and processing information to generate the necessary output.
Portable hard drive	20 GB to 120 GB	Storing large amounts of data, including audio and video
Rewritable CD, or CD-RW	650 MB	Recording and re-recording data on the same CD-ROM

Do it!

C-2: Discussing other removable storage devices

Questions and answers

1 Name some storage devices other than CD-ROMs and DVDs.

2 Sandra wants to use a storage device for her laptop. Which device would you suggest?

3 If you want to copy 150 MB of data from your office computer for use at home, which storage device would you use?

4 Which storage device would you use to store large picture files?

4–14 Introduction to Personal Computers

Unit summary: Data storage

Topic A   In this topic, you learned how to **write-protect** and **format** a **floppy disk**.

Topic B   In this topic, you learned about **hard disks** and how to check the **capacity** of a hard disk.

Topic C   In this topic, you learned about some other storage devices: **CD-ROMs, DVDs, Click disks, keydrives, SuperDisks, Zip disks, Optical disks, Magnetic strips, Smart cards, portable hard drives,** and **rewritable CDs**.

Independent practice activity

1 Write-protect your floppy disk.

2 Format your floppy disk by using the format type called **Quick Format**. (Notice that there is an error message that you cannot format the floppy disk because it is write-protected.)

3 Remove write-protection.

4 Format the floppy disk.

5 Close the Format 3 1/2 Floppy (A:) dialog box and close the My Computer window.

6 Remove the floppy disk from the floppy drive.

Review questions

1 Which storage device is best suited to transferring small amounts of data between computers?

2 How can you ensure that data stored on a floppy disk is not deleted or overwritten?

3 Why is a hard disk less prone to damage compared to a floppy disk?

4 What details of the hard disk does its Properties dialog box display?

Data storage   **4–15**

5 List two storage devices, other than a floppy disk, on which you can write data.

6 What is the advantage of using a hard disk over a floppy disk?

7 How are DVDs different from CD-ROMs?

4–16 Introduction to Personal Computers

Unit 5
Output devices

Unit time: 35 minutes

Complete this unit, and you'll know how to:

A Apply monitor and desktop layout settings.

B Discuss other output devices such as printers, plotters, and sound cards.

5–2 Introduction to Personal Computers

Topic A: Monitor and desktop layout basics

Explanation

The most common output devices are monitors, printers, and plotters. You use these devices to see the information processed by a computer. A sound card is another commonly used output device that helps you obtain sound output on speakers attached to your computer.

Monitors

Monitors are classified according to the features they support. Some of these features are:

- **Support for color**. Monitors can be classified as monochrome or colored. *Monochrome monitors* can display only two colors, one for the foreground and the other for the background. *Color monitors* can display hundreds to millions of colors.

- **Size**. The size of a monitor is measured diagonally across the screen. Monitors are available in various sizes, ranging from 14 inches to 24 inches, with 17-inch monitors being used most commonly. Large monitors of 19 inches and 21 inches are increasingly becoming more affordable for computer users.

Resolution

The display screen of a monitor is considered to be an array of tiny dots called *pixels* (or picture elements). Anything that appears on the screen is displayed using these pixels. A pixel can be on or off. If a pixel is on, it appears on the screen. If a pixel is off, it doesn't appear on the screen.

The two factors that determine the quality of display are:

- *Resolution*. The number of pixels that appear on the screen. The default resolution is usually determined by the computer manufacturer, and is related to the display adapter (card) and the monitor that come with the computer system. Common screen resolutions used today are 1024×768 and 800×600 pixels. Monitors that can handle resolutions up to 1280×768 pixels are also available.

- *Dot pitch*. The distance between two pixels. As the dot pitch decreases, the sharpness of the text or image displayed increases.

You can change the resolution of a monitor to display more information on the screen by choosing 1024×768 pixels. To change the screen resolution, you need to right-click the blank area on the desktop and choose Properties. Next, in the Display Properties dialog box (shown in Exhibit 5-1), click the Settings tab and drag the Screen resolution slider to 1024 by 768 pixels.

Output devices **5–3**

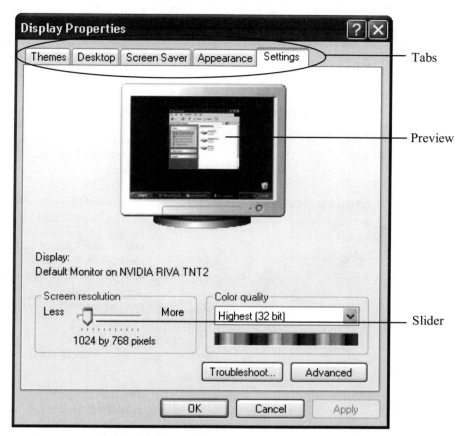

Exhibit 5-1: A sample Display Properties dialog box

5–4 Introduction to Personal Computers

Do it!

A-1: Changing the monitor resolution

Here's how	Here's why
1 Right-click anywhere in the blank area on the desktop	To display a shortcut menu.
Choose **Properties**	To open the Display Properties dialog box.
Observe the dialog box	It contains the Themes, Desktop, Screen Saver, Appearance, and Settings tabs. The Themes tab is selected by default.
2 Click the **Settings** tab	To activate the tab. You'll use this tab to change the resolution of your monitor (as shown in Exhibit 5-1.) The dialog box also displays a picture of a monitor called Preview, which shows how the monitor will appear after applying the settings you select.
Observe the Screen resolution area	Screen resolution Less — More 1024 by 768 pixels
	The slider is positioned at 1024 by 768 pixels, indicating that the resolution is currently 1024×768 pixels. To choose other resolutions, drag the slider along the scale.
3 Drag the slider to **800 by 600 pixels**	Screen resolution Less — More 800 by 600 pixels
	To change the resolution to 800×600 pixels.
Click **Apply**	The screen flickers and the resolution changes. A confirmation box might appear, asking you to confirm if you want to retain the new setting for the desktop. It also displays a countdown clock starting at 15 seconds, which is the time you can take to confirm the new settings.
4 Click **No**	(If required.) To revert to the previous resolution.

Output devices **5–5**

Desktop background and screensavers

Explanation

To change the appearance of the desktop, you can change its background and use screensavers. When you change the background, the icons on the desktop will remain in the foreground while the image selected will form a background. You can either choose from the range of background images provided by Windows XP, or specify any image stored on your computer as the background. To change the background, click the Desktop tab in the Display Properties dialog box. Next, select a background image and its position and click OK.

A *screensaver* is a utility that displays text or graphics on the screen when your computer is idle for a specified time. Pressing a key or moving the mouse deactivates the screensaver.

Do it!

A-2: Using desktop background and screensavers

Here's how	Here's why
1 In the Display Properties dialog box, activate the Desktop tab	Click it.
2 Under Background, select **Blue Lace 16**	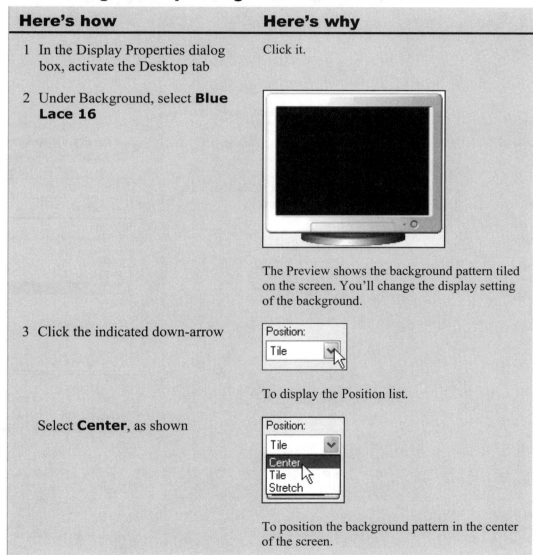 The Preview shows the background pattern tiled on the screen. You'll change the display setting of the background.
3 Click the indicated down-arrow	To display the Position list.
Select **Center**, as shown	To position the background pattern in the center of the screen.

4	Observe the Preview	
		It shows the background pattern in the center of the screen.
5	Click **OK**	The Display Properties dialog box closes, and the selected background image appears in the center of the screen.
6	Open the Display Properties dialog box	Right-click the desktop, and from the shortcut menu, choose Properties.
7	Activate the Screen Saver tab	
8	Display the Screen saver list	Click the down-arrow to the right of the current screensaver to display the Screen saver list.
	From the Screen saver list, select **Beziers**, as shown	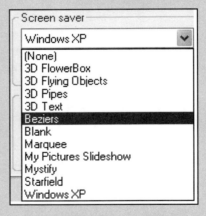
	Observe the dialog box	The Preview shows the Beziers screensaver. The screensaver appears if you don't use the mouse or keyboard for a specified time, which is 10 minutes by default. You can change this setting.
9	Click **Preview**	To see how the screen will appear when the selected screensaver is activated. Do not move the mouse or press a key on the keyboard.
10	Move the mouse	To deactivate the screensaver.
11	Click **OK**	To apply the selected screensaver and close the Display Properties dialog box.

Output devices **5-7**

Explanation

Topic B: Other output devices

You use printers and plotters to create hard copies of the information stored on a computer. To hear the sound effects in multimedia programs and listen to music on your computer, you use a sound card and speakers.

Types of printers

Many types of printers are available today. Each type of printer has special features associated with it. Printers are classified based on their features, such as speed, quality, and direction of printing. When choosing a printer, you should be clear about your needs in terms of the following features:

- Speed
- Print quality
- Cost

The following table describes some of the most commonly used printers.

Printer	Description
Laser	Produces high-quality output, both in text and graphics. It's suitable for printing business correspondence, newsletters, and brochures. You can also use a laser printer for printing on envelopes and cards. It is available in either color or black-and-white and costs more than an inkjet printer.
Inkjet	Produces high quality print but is slow in performance. It is the best option if you want high-resolution color printouts. It's available in either color or black-and-white and costs less than a laser printer.
Dot matrix	Produces low-quality print as compared to the other two types of printers. It's also the oldest of the three types of printers. Dot matrix printers are used when print quality is not crucial, such as for reports and memos to be printed for internal circulation within an organization.

Do it!

B-1: Discussing types of printers

Questions and answers

1 List some of the factors that determine the type of printer you choose to buy.

2 David wants to print invitation cards for a party. Which printer is most suitable for his requirement?

3 Which printer is the best option for creating high-resolution color printouts?

5–8   Introduction to Personal Computers

Plotters

Explanation

A *plotter* is an output device that uses a pen to print output on large sheets of paper. It produces continuous lines unlike a printer, which simulates lines by printing a series of dots. Therefore, plotters are used to print high-quality visuals, charts, graphs, tables, and diagrams. For example, you use plotters to print architectural plans and engineering drawings, where high precision is required. Plotters are more expensive than printers.

Plotters are divided into two broad categories, flatbed and drum. In a flatbed plotter, the paper is held stationary while the pen moves over it. In contrast, in the drum plotter the paper is wrapped around a drum and anchored at both ends. The drum rotates while the pen moves laterally.

Do it!

B-2:   Discussing plotters

Questions and answers

1   Jane needs to print an architectural plan for a mall. Which output device will she use?

2   What are the two main types of plotters?

Output devices   **5–9**

Sound cards

Explanation

A sound card, also known as a sound board, is an output device that processes digital information stored in sound files and sends this information to speakers or headphones to produce sounds. The most frequently used sound files are WAV (pronounced "wave") files, MP3 files, and audio files. The sound card can be used for the following purposes:

- To capture audio from another external sound device attached to it, such as a radio or a TV, and save that audio on the computer hard drive.
- To facilitate two-way audio communication on the Internet.
- To capture words through microphones, transfer them to a voice word processor, and display them on the monitor.

Do it!

B-3: Discussing sound card basics

Question and answer
1 What is a sound card?
2 Name some of the most frequently used sound files.
3 For what purposes can a sound card be used?

5–10   Introduction to Personal Computers

Unit summary: Output devices

Topic A   In this topic, you learned about the different types of **monitors** and their features. You also learned how to set a **background** on a desktop and apply a **screensaver**.

Topic B   In this topic, you learned that you can use **printers** to obtain printed copies of documents. You also learned that you use **plotters** to print high-quality prints. Finally, you learned about **sound card** basics.

Independent practice activity

1 Open the Display Properties dialog box.

2 Select a desktop background of your choice.

3 Apply the new desktop background.

4 Set the screensaver as **Starfield**.

5 Preview the screensaver.

6 Apply the screensaver.

7 Close the Display Properties dialog box.

Review questions

1 What is the difference between resolution and dot pitch?

2 When the dot pitch decreases, does the image become sharper or blurrier?

3 Which of the following statements is true for a 17-inch monitor?

A It measures 17 inches wide.

B It measures 17 inches high.

C It measures 17 inches in area.

D It measures 17 inches diagonally.

4 Which Display Properties dialog box tab should you use to change the screen resolution?

5 What is the advantage of a screensaver?

6 What are the three types of printers?

Unit 6

Managing data

Unit time: 70 minutes

Complete this unit, and you'll know how to:

A Use Windows Explorer to browse the computer hard disk.

B Create and rename folders.

C Create and print files.

D Protect your computer from viruses.

Topic A: Working with Windows Explorer

Explanation

The basic unit of storage on a computer is a *file*. In a filing cabinet, you store your files in a folder (as shown in Exhibit 6-1). Files stored on your computer are also organized in *folders*. Folders can also store other folders. A folder stored within another folder is called a *subfolder*.

You can store files and folders in specific locations in a folder hierarchy, making it easy to identify where a particular file or folder is located. The folder at the top of the hierarchy in a storage device, such as a hard disk or a floppy disk, is called the *root folder* (root). This folder contains all the other folders and their subfolders. The root folder on the hard disk is denoted by C:, and the root folder on the floppy disk is denoted by A:.

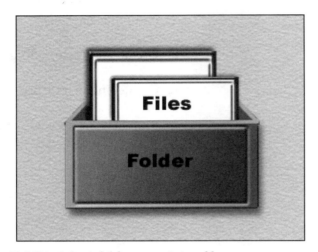

Exhibit 6-1: A folder containing files

To access a file, you need to know its name and location. The location of a file or a folder is referred to as its *path* or *address*. In a path, the name of the root folder, other folders, subfolders, and the file are separated by back slashes (\). For example, the path of the file "Myfile.txt" stored in the folder "Myproject," which is stored in C: is:

    C:\Myproject\Myfile.txt

You can use Windows Explorer, a Windows XP program, to view the contents of a computer in a hierarchy. You can then navigate to any file stored on the hard disk, a floppy disk, or a CD-ROM.

The Windows Explorer window

To start Windows Explorer, click Start, and then choose All Programs, Accessories, Windows Explorer. Windows Explorer is divided into two sections called *panes*. The left pane displays a hierarchical view of the disks (these include the hard disk, floppy disk, and CD-ROM) and folders on your computer. The right pane displays the contents of the disk or folder that is selected in the left pane, as shown in Exhibit 6-2. You can change the width of each pane by dragging the divider to the right or the left.

Like other Windows-based applications, the Windows Explorer window has a menu bar and a toolbar at the top in the window, as shown in Exhibit 6-2. A menu bar provides options for accessing the features of the application. Each item on the menu bar has a submenu. A toolbar contains buttons for tasks that are performed frequently.

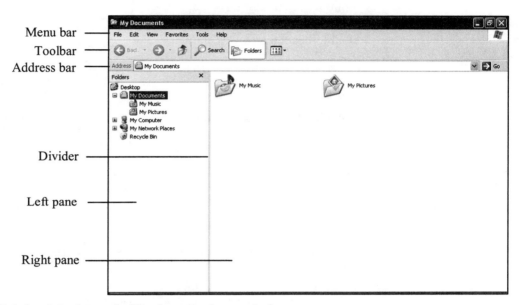

Exhibit 6-2: A sample Windows Explorer window

Expanding and collapsing the folder hierarchy

You can expand and collapse the folder hierarchy structure in the left pane of the Windows Explorer window. A plus sign (+) next to a folder name indicates that the folder contains subfolders, and it can be expanded. A minus sign (−) next to a folder name indicates that the folder cannot be expanded any further. You can click these symbols to expand or collapse a folder.

6–4 Introduction to Personal Computers

Do it!

A-1: Expanding and collapsing a folder

Here's how	Here's why
1 Click **Start**	To display the Start menu.
Choose **All Programs**, **Accessories**, **Windows Explorer**	To start Windows Explorer. The window is divided into two sections called panes.
2 Maximize the window	(If necessary.) On the right side of the title bar, click the middle button.
3 Point to the divider until the mouse pointer shape changes to a double-headed arrow as shown	The double-headed arrow indicates that you can drag the divider to either side.
Drag the divider to the right	To increase the width of the left pane. This is helpful for seeing long names of disks and folders.
4 Observe the folder icons in the left pane	A plus sign (+) indicates that the folder contains subfolders that aren't currently displayed. A minus sign (–) indicates that all the subfolders in the folder are displayed.
5 Observe the plus sign (+) next to My Computer	It indicates that the My Computer folder is currently collapsed. None of its subfolders are visible.
6 Click [+]	To expand the My Computer folder hierarchy. The plus sign (+) changes to a minus sign (–), and the folder hierarchy in My Computer appears in the left pane.
7 Locate Local Disk (C:)	This is the root folder of the hard disk.

Managing data   **6–5**

Navigating the folder hierarchy

Explanation   Navigating the folder hierarchy is the activity of locating specific files and folders. You can use the left and right panes of Windows Explorer to find a file or a folder. You can also use the Address bar (shown in Exhibit 6-2) located directly above the panes. The Address bar displays your current location in the folder hierarchy.

Do it!   ## A-2:   Navigating with Windows Explorer

Here's how	Here's why
1 In the left pane, click **Local Disk (C:)**	To display the files and subfolders of Local Disk (C:) in the right pane. You'll navigate to the Accessories folder.
2 In the right pane, double-click **Program Files**	To display the files and subfolders of the Program Files folder in the right pane.
In the right pane, double-click **Windows NT**	The files and folders stored within Windows NT are listed in the right pane.
In the right pane, double-click **Accessories**	You can see the files stored in the Accessories folder.
3 Observe the Address bar	

Address   C:\Program Files\Windows NT\Accessories

It displays the location of the selected folder in the hierarchy. (If the Accessories folder is located in the Program Files folder instead, the pictured path will be different on your computer: C:\Program Files\Accessories.)

6–6 Introduction to Personal Computers

Topic B: Working with folders

Explanation

You can organize your files by creating folders on a computer desktop, a hard disk, a floppy disk, or any other storage device. When you create a folder, you assign it a name. You can also rename a folder.

Creating folders

You can store your files in an existing folder or create a new folder to keep them organized. To create a folder at the current location in the folder hierarchy, in Windows Explorer, choose File, New, Folder. You can also right-click anywhere on the blank area in the Windows Explorer window and choose New, Folder from the shortcut menu.

Folder naming conventions

After you create a new folder, you need to assign a name to it. A folder name can contain up to 255 characters, including spaces. However, you should try to keep the names short, simple, and meaningful so that they are easy to remember. A folder name can contain any characters except for the following:

    \ / : * ? " < > |

Do it!

B-1: Creating a folder

Here's how	Here's why
1 In the left pane, click **Local Disk (C:)**	
2 Choose **File, New, Folder**	A new folder appears, with the default name "New Folder." The folder's name is selected so that you can specify another name.
3 Type **Myfolder**	The new name "Myfolder" will replace the text "New Folder."
Press (↵ ENTER)	To assign the name to the folder. The new name appears only after you press Enter or click elsewhere on the screen.
4 Observe the left pane	The folder "Myfolder" is added to the list of folders under Local Disk (C:).
In the left pane, click **Myfolder**	The right pane is empty, which means that this folder doesn't contain any subfolders or files.

Managing data **6–7**

Renaming folders

Explanation

Renaming a folder is the process of changing the name of an existing folder. You might need to rename a folder whenever you modify the folder's contents. For example, suppose you created a folder named Mydetails that contained files related only to you. Later, you added files related to your team members as well. As a result, you might want to change the name of the folder to Teamdetails to indicate the wider range of information stored in this location. To rename a folder, you need to ensure that it's selected in Windows Explorer. Next, choose File, Rename. The folder's name is selected to indicate that you can enter a new name for it.

Do it!

B-2:   Renaming a folder

Here's how	Here's why
1 Choose **File**, **Rename**	
2 Observe the left pane	The folder's name is selected.
3 Enter **Mywork**	(Type Mywork and press Enter.) To rename the folder. The new name "Mywork" replaces the old name "Myfolder."
4 Choose **File**, **Close**	To close Windows Explorer.

6–8 Introduction to Personal Computers

Topic C: Working with files

Explanation

In your day-to-day life, you might store information in the form of paper files. You can also store information on a computer by creating files. A file, once created, can be printed. You can also move a file or store a copy of a file in another location on a hard disk or a floppy disk.

If you no longer need a file, you can delete it. When you delete a file, the file moves to the *Recycle Bin*, a folder located on the hard disk. You can either delete the file permanently from the Recycle Bin or restore the file to its original location on the hard disk. You can also search for a file if you are unable to recall its name or location after creating it.

The procedures for moving, copying, deleting, restoring, and searching for a folder are the same as those for a file.

Creating and saving files

When creating a file, you can save it in a specific location on the hard disk by designating a path for the file. The naming convention used for files is the same as that for folders. Every file has an *extension*, three characters to the right of the file name, which indicates the type of application used to create it. For example, when you create a new file by using Notepad, Windows XP appends the extension ".txt" to the end of the file name. Therefore, if you save the Notepad file with the name Myfile, Windows XP saves it as Myfile.txt.

The Save As dialog box

The first time you save a document, you'll need to use the Save As dialog box (as shown in Exhibit 6-3) to assign a name to the document and specify a location in which to save the file.

Often, you'll make changes to an existing document then save it with the same name at the same location. This action is called an *update* and you need not interact with the Save As dialog box in this case.

Exhibit 6-3: The Save As dialog box

6–10 Introduction to Personal Computers

Do it!

C-1: Creating and saving a file on the hard disk

Here's how	Here's why
1 Click **Start**	
Choose **All Programs**, **Accessories**, **Notepad**	To open a new file with the default name "Untitled."
2 Type your name	
3 Choose **File**, **Save As...**	To open the Save As dialog box.
Observe the Save As dialog box	(As shown in Exhibit 6-3.) The dialog box appears the first time you save a document. The extension, *.txt, appears highlighted in the File name box. You can start typing to assign a file name. The Save in box shows the My Documents folder, which is the default location for saving a file.
In the File name box, enter **Myfile**	File name: Myfile
	To specify Myfile as the name of your file in the File name box.
4 Click the Save in box down-arrow as indicated	Save in: My Documents / My Recent Documents / Desktop / My Documents / My Computer / 3½ Floppy (A:) / Local Disk (C:) / CD Drive (D:) / My Network Places
	A list of folders that are stored on the desktop appears. You can navigate to any folder by clicking its name.
From the list, select **Local Disk (C:)**	To display a list of folders stored on Local Disk (C:) in the window below the Save in list. You can store the file in the root or navigate to a specific folder.
5 Double-click **Mywork**	To specify this folder as the location for saving the file "Myfile."
Click **Save**	
Observe the title bar	The name of the file "Myfile" appears.

Managing data   **6-11**

6 Press ⏎ ENTER   To move to the next line.

   Type your address

   Choose **File**, **Save**   To update the file.

7 Type your telephone number   Press Enter to move to the next line and type.
   below your address

   Choose **File**, **Exit**

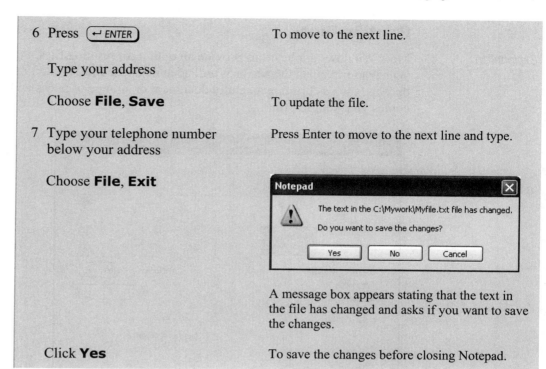

                                A message box appears stating that the text in
                                the file has changed and asks if you want to save
                                the changes.

   Click **Yes**   To save the changes before closing Notepad.

Printing files

Explanation

Most Windows applications provide an option for printing files. For example, to print a WordPad file, open the file in WordPad and choose File, Print. You can specify several options, such as printing an entire document or a range of pages and the number of copies you want to print.

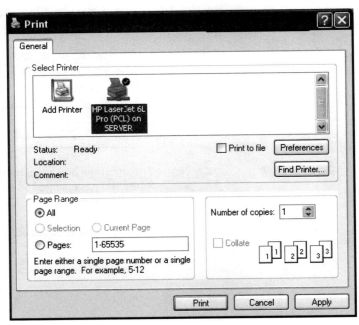

Exhibit 6-4: A sample Print dialog box

Do it!

C-2: Printing a file

Here's how	Here's why
1 Open WordPad	Click Start, choose All Programs, Accessories, WordPad.
2 Type the names and addresses of two of your friends	
3 Choose **File**, **Save As...**	To open the Save As dialog box. In the Save as type box, Rich Text Format (RTF) is automatically selected as the file format for a WordPad file.
In the File name box, enter **Myfriends**	To specify Myfriends as the name of your file.
Click **Save**	To save the file "Myfriends" in the default folder "My Documents."
4 Choose **File**, **Print...**	To open the Print dialog box (a sample dialog box is shown in Exhibit 6-4).
Observe the dialog box	Under Select Printer, the default printer is selected. Under Page Range, "All" is selected, indicating that all the pages in the document will be printed by default. You can also designate specific pages that you want to print. In the list next to Number of copies, 1 appears by default, indicating that one copy is printed unless otherwise specified.
5 Click **Cancel**	To close the Print dialog box without printing.
6 Choose **File**, **Exit**	To close the file and WordPad.

6–14 Introduction to Personal Computers

Moving files

Explanation
While working in Windows XP, you frequently need to organize files and folders by moving and copying them. When you copy a file (or a folder), you create its duplicate at another location in the hierarchy. The original file or folder remains unchanged. However, when you move a file, you remove the file from its original location to a new location.

To move a file from one folder to another:

1 Click the file that you want to move.

2 Choose Edit, Cut.

3 Navigate to the destination folder.

4 Choose Edit, Paste.

To copy a file:

1 Select the file.

2 Choose Edit, Copy.

3 Navigate to the destination folder.

4 Choose Edit, Paste.

Do it!
C-3: Moving a file

Here's how	Here's why
1 Start Windows Explorer	Click Start, choose All Programs, Windows Explorer.
2 In the left pane of Windows Explorer, navigate to **C:\Mywork**	(If necessary.) To view the files located in this folder. One file, Myfile, is contained within this folder and appears in the right pane.
In the right pane, select **Myfile**	(Click the file name.) You'll move this file to the root of Local Drive (C:).
3 Choose **Edit, Cut**	To use the menu method to cut the file from its current location. The icon associated with the file name appears dimmed, indicating that the file is removed from its current location.
4 In the left pane, select **Local Disk (C:)**	To view the contents of the C:\ folder in the right pane of the Explorer window.
5 Choose **Edit, Paste**	To use the menu method to paste the file at the new location.
6 Observe the right pane	Myfile is moved to the C:\ folder.
7 In the left pane, navigate to **C:\Mywork**	Notice that "Myfile" is no longer present in this folder.

Managing data   **6–15**

Copying files to floppy disks

Explanation

You can also copy files and folders to a floppy disk. When you store a copy of a file in a different location than the original file, the copy is called a *backup*. Storing a backup of a file is highly recommended. It ensures that if something happens to the original file, perhaps it's accidentally deleted or becomes corrupted for some reason, the information is preserved in another file stored in a separate location, such as a floppy disk.

To copy a file to a floppy disk, point to the file, right-click, and choose Send To, 3 1/2 Floppy (A:).

Do it!

C-4:   Copying a file to a floppy disk

Here's how	Here's why
1 Insert the floppy disk in the floppy disk drive	If necessary.
2 In the left pane of Windows Explorer, select **Local Disk (C:)**	This is the folder containing the file Myfile. You should see the file in the right pane.
3 In the right pane, right-click **Myfile**	To display a shortcut menu. You'll copy the file to the floppy disk.
Choose **Send To**, **3 1/2 Floppy (A:)**, as shown	Open Print Edit Open With ▶ **Send To** ▶ 📁 Compressed (zipped) Folder Cut 📇 Desktop (create shortcut) Copy 📄 Mail Recipient Create Shortcut 📄 My Documents Delete 💾 3½ Floppy (A:) Rename Properties
4 In the left pane, select **3 1/2 Floppy (A:)**	Myfile appears in the right pane indicating that it is copied to the floppy disk.

Deleting files

Explanation

You might want to delete files if you no longer need them. When you delete a file, it's moved to the Recycle Bin folder. If you want to permanently delete a file from your computer, you'll have to delete it from the Recycle Bin folder.

To delete a file, select the file and use any of the following methods:

- Press the Delete key.
- Choose File, Delete.
- From the shortcut menu, choose Delete.

Do it!

C-5: Deleting a file

Here's how	Here's why
1 In Local Disk (C:), select **Myfile**	(In the left pane, select Local Disk (C:) and then in the right pane, select Myfile.) You'll delete this file.
2 Press (DELETE) 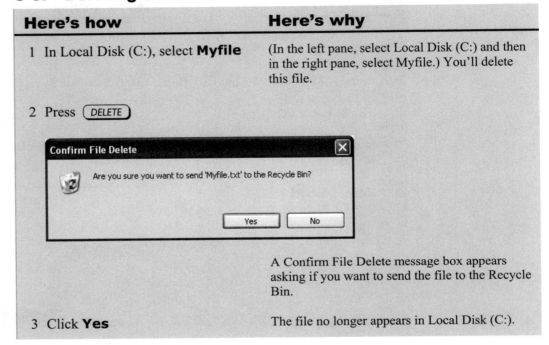	A Confirm File Delete message box appears asking if you want to send the file to the Recycle Bin.
3 Click **Yes**	The file no longer appears in Local Disk (C:).

Managing data   **6–17**

Restoring files

Explanation

If a file is in the Recycle Bin, you can restore that file to its original location. To restore a file, you can use the following two methods:

- In the Recycle Bin folder, select the file and choose File, Restore.
- In the Recycle Bin folder, right-click the file and from the shortcut menu, choose Restore.

Do it!

C-6:   Restoring a file

Here's how	Here's why
1 In the left pane, select **Recycle Bin**	The Myfile text document appears in the right pane. You'll restore this document.
2 In the right pane, select **Myfile**	
3 Choose **File, Restore**	The Myfile text document disappears from the right pane.
4 In the left pane, select **Local Disk (C:)**	The Myfile text document is restored to the root folder from which it was deleted.

6–18 Introduction to Personal Computers

Searching for files

Explanation

If you have saved a file and cannot remember the file name or the location where you saved it, you can search for the file by using the Search feature of Windows.

To use the Search feature, click the Search button on the toolbar. The left pane of Windows Explorer changes to display the Search feature called *Search Companion*, as shown in Exhibit 6-5. It contains various options that you can use to search for files, folders, and printers. For example, let's say you saved a file created using WordPad on drive C. However, you can't remember the exact location of the file on the drive. To search for the file, select the All files and folders option and type the file name in the All or part of the file name text box. Next, ensure that Local Disk (C:) is selected in the Look in box and then click the Search button.

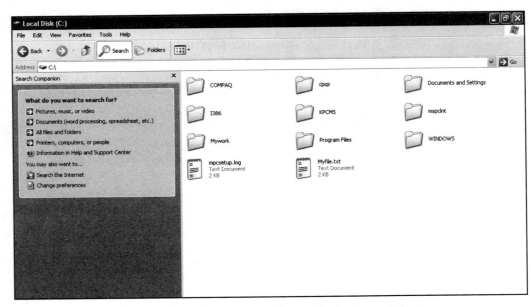

Exhibit 6-5: A sample Windows Explorer window with the Search feature

Do it!

C-7: Searching for a file

Here's how	Here's why
1 Click the **Search** button	⌕ Search (On the toolbar.) To open the Search feature.
Observe the Windows Explorer window	The left pane changes to display the Search feature "Search Companion."

Managing data   **6–19**

2 Select **All files and folders**

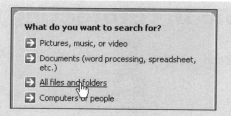

Observe the Search Companion pane

It displays several search criteria. For example, you can search for a file by specifying its name. Or you can search by specifying the date and time when you last worked on the file or the file size. The Look in box displays the current folder, Local Disk (C:), as the default location to be searched.

3 In the All or part of the file name box, enter **Myfriends**   To search for the file Myfriends on drive C:.

4 Click **Search**

Observe the Search Companion pane   The Search Companion pane shows a message indicating the file it's searching for, the location where it's searching, and the status of the search.

Observe the right pane   The right pane displays the result of the search.

5 Click **Stop**   (If necessary.) To stop running the Search feature.

6 Click ☒   (In the upper-right corner of the Windows Explorer window.) To close Windows Explorer.

6–20 Introduction to Personal Computers

Topic D: Protecting data against viruses

Explanation

A *virus* is a set of instructions (a program) that is designed to interrupt the operations of a computer or damage the data and programs on it. The amount of damage caused varies from one virus to another. Some viruses cause damage very quickly while others remain dormant for some time. The nature of damage also varies. They might interrupt your work by displaying messages, delete or corrupt files on the hard disk, or change file sizes.

Viruses can transmit to a computer via portable storage devices, such as floppy disks and Zip disks, the Internet, or e-mail. For example, a virus can transmit to a computer through an infected floppy disk when you copy or delete files from the disk. Some viruses infect your computer only if you start the computer with an infected floppy disk inserted in the drive.

A virus copies itself into a file called the *host*. It then creates multiple copies of itself on different locations of the hard disk. Depending on the type of virus, it might infect all files on the hard disk, a specific application, or the operating system.

You can avoid losing data stored on your hard disk, should a virus infect your computer, by making regular backups. If you are using a floppy disk to retrieve information stored on it, you can write-protect it to ensure that a virus does not infect the floppy disk. There are many antivirus programs available that can detect and clean viruses. Two popular antivirus programs are McAfee and Norton. You should install an antivirus program on your computer to ensure that a virus does not infect it.

Do it!

D-1: Discussing viruses

Questions and answers
1 How might you know that a virus has infected your computer?
2 List two ways in which a virus might be transferred to your computer.
3 How can you prevent your computer from being infected by viruses?

Managing data   **6–21**

Unit summary: Managing data

Topic A
In this topic, you learned that data is stored in **files**. Each file is stored in a **folder**. Files and folders are organized in a **folder hierarchy**, with Local Drive (C:) as the root folder. You also learned how to navigate the folder hierarchy by using **Windows Explorer**.

Topic B
In this topic, you learned how to **create** a folder. You also learned how to **rename** a folder.

Topic C
In this topic, you learned how to **save**, **print**, **move**, **copy**, **delete**, **restore**, and **search** files.

Topic D
In this topic, you learned how **viruses** can affect a computer and how **antivirus programs** can protect your computer from them.

Independent practice activity

1   Open Windows Explorer.

2   On drive C:, create a new folder called **Mypractice** folder.

3   Create a new document by using Notepad.

4   Type a short message in the document.

5   Save the document as **Practice** in the C:\Mypractice folder.

6   Close Notepad.

7   Move Practice to My Documents. (The My Documents folder is under "Desktop.")

8   Copy Practice to the floppy disk.

9   In the My Documents folder, delete Practice.

10   Restore Practice to its original location.

11   Search for all files named Practice.

12   Close Windows Explorer.

Review questions

1   In the folder hierarchy, what do you call the very top of the hierarchy?

2   Which letter usually denotes the root folder?

3   Which letter usually denotes the floppy disk drive?

4   In Windows Explorer, what does the plus (*) sign indicate?

6–22 Introduction to Personal Computers

5 Which of the following can folder names contain?

A ?

B space

C *

D /

6 If you mistakenly delete a file, how can you get it back?

7 Which of the following actions enables you to create a backup of a file on a floppy disk?

A Save

B Print

C Move

D Copy

Unit 7

Working with applications

Unit time: 130 minutes

Complete this unit, and you'll know how to:

A Use Windows XP Accessories.

B Work with Outlook Express.

C Work with Internet Explorer 6.0.

D Access Help and Support and shut down a computer.

Topic A: Windows XP Accessories

Explanation

Windows XP provides several programs called *Accessories*. Although you can use more robust software packages to accomplish much of your work, Windows XP Accessories come in handy when you need to do small, informal tasks. Three of the most useful accessories are WordPad, Calculator, and Paint.

WordPad

WordPad (as shown in Exhibit 7-1) is a simple and efficient word processor. You can use WordPad to create, edit, format, and print simple documents. To start WordPad, click Start, and then choose All Programs, Accessories, WordPad.

In WordPad, you create a new document by choosing File, New or by clicking the New button on the toolbar.

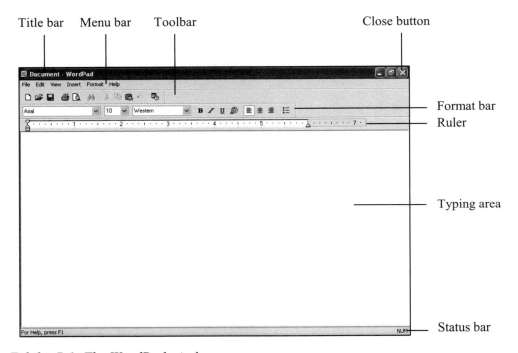

Exhibit 7-1: The WordPad window

Editing a document

After you enter text in a document, you can make changes to it. You can edit the contents of your document by inserting, deleting, or replacing text. However, before you can edit text, you must select it. To do so, click and hold the mouse button and drag it over the text. You can select a specific word by double-clicking it. The following table summarizes some basic editing techniques.

To...	Procedure
Insert text	Place the mouse pointer at the position you want to insert text, then click the mouse button and begin typing.
Replace selected text	Select the text and then type the new text.
Delete selected text	Select the text and then press the Backspace or the Delete key on the keyboard.
Delete characters	Place the insertion point to the right of the text to be deleted, and then press the Backspace key until the text is deleted. You can also place the insertion point to the left of the text to be deleted and then press the Delete key until the text is deleted.
Move selected text	Select the text and drag it to the required position in your document.

Formatting a document

Formatting a document refers to changing the appearance of its contents. For example, you can change the size or font of the text in your document. You can also bold, italicize, or underline text. To apply formatting, you can use the Format bar or choose Format, Font from the menu bar. When you choose the command from the menu bar, the Font dialog box appears, as shown in Exhibit 7-2.

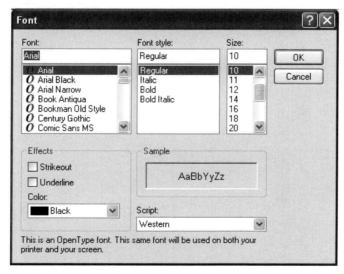

Exhibit 7-2: The Font dialog box

Introduction to Personal Computers

The Format bar (as shown in Exhibit 7-3) provides most of the options available in the Font dialog box.

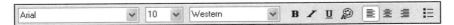

Exhibit 7-3: The Format bar

The following table describes the buttons and other elements available on the Format bar.

Element	Name	Description
Arial	Font box	Changes the font style of the selected text.
10	Font Size box	Changes the size of the selected text. You can either click in the box and enter the font size or select the font size from the list.
Western	Font Script box	Selects the language script available for the selected font.
B	Bold button	Bolds the selected text.
I	Italic button	Italicizes the selected text.
U	Underline button	Underlines the selected text.
(palette)	Color button	Displays the various colors you can apply to selected text. To apply a color to the selected text, click this button and select the desired color from the drop-down list.
(align left icon)	Align Left button	Left aligns the selected text.
(center icon)	Center button	Centers the selected text.
(align right icon)	Align Right button	Right aligns selected text.
(bullets icon)	Bullets button	Converts the selected text to a bulleted list.

Do it!

A-1: Working with WordPad

Here's how	Here's why
1 Start WordPad	Click Start, and then choose All Programs, Accessories, WordPad.
2 Click ▣	(In the upper-right corner of the WordPad window, if necessary.) To enlarge, or "maximize," the WordPad window to cover the computer screen.
3 Type **Introduction to WordPad**	
Press ⏎ ENTER twice	To move the insertion point down two lines to create a blank line in the document.
4 Type **WordPad is easy to use.**	
5 Drag over the text **Introduction to WordPad** as shown	Introduction to WordPad
	To select the text.
6 Click the Font drop-down arrow as indicated	Arial
	(On the Format bar.) To view the list of available fonts.
7 Observe the scroll bar	(On the right side of the Font list.) When a list is too long to be displayed in its entirety, you can drag the scroll box in the scroll bar to view remaining items.
Drag the scroll box down as shown	Arial O Arial O Arial Black O Arial Narrow O Arial Rounded MT Bold O Blackadder ITC
	To view additional items in the list.
Select **Verdana** as shown	O Times New Roman O Trebuchet MS O Tunga O Verdana O Webdings O Wingdings T Wingdings 2 T Wingdings 3
	The font of the selected text changes.

7–6   Introduction to Personal Computers

8	Click the Font Size drop-down arrow	(On the Format bar.) To view the various font sizes available.
	Select **14**	To increase the size of the selected text.
9	Click **B**	To bold the selected text.
10	Click *I*	To italicize the selected text.
11	Click <u>U</u>	To underline the selected text.
12	Click ≣	To center the selected text on the page.
13	Click 💾	(On the toolbar.) To save the changes made to the document. The Save As dialog box appears.
	Under Local Disk (C:)\Mywork, save the file as **Mydocument**	
14	Click ✕	(In the upper-right corner of the WordPad window.) To close WordPad.

Working with applications   **7–7**

Calculator

Explanation

Just as you use a pocket calculator for simple calculations, Windows XP provides an application called Calculator that you can use to perform mathematical calculations. To open Calculator, click Start, and then choose All Programs, Accessories, Calculator. Calculator has two views, Standard and Scientific. Both views have a display area to show the input and the result. The Standard view provides simple operators, such as addition (+), subtraction (–), multiplication (*), division (/), and square root. You use the Scientific view to perform scientific calculations. By default, Calculator opens in the Standard view. To switch to Scientific view, choose View, Scientific.

Do it!

A-2:   Working with Calculator

Here's how	Here's why
1 Click **Start**	
Choose **All Programs**, **Accessories**, **Calculator**	To open Calculator. You'll calculate the product of 25 and 35.
2 Click [2]	To select the first digit of the first input, which is "25." Notice that "2" appears in the blank area below the menu, called the display area.
Click [5]	`|                                                    25. |`
	To select the second digit of the first input. Now "25" appears in the display area.
3 Click [*]	To select the multiplication operator.
4 In the display area, enter **35**	(You can click the numbers 3 and 5 on the Calculator's keypad, or you can type the numbers.) This is the second input.
5 Click [=]	To perform the calculation. The product of 25 and 35 is 875, and it appears in the display area.
Close Calculator	Click the Close button in the upper-right corner of the Calculator window.

Paint

Explanation

Paint is a graphics program that is available with Windows XP. Paint provides several tools for creating drawings, designs, and images that you can use in other Windows programs. To start Paint, click Start, and then choose All Programs, Accessories, Paint. The insertion point that appears in the drawing area of the Paint window resembles a pencil. Exhibit 7-4 shows a sample Paint window.

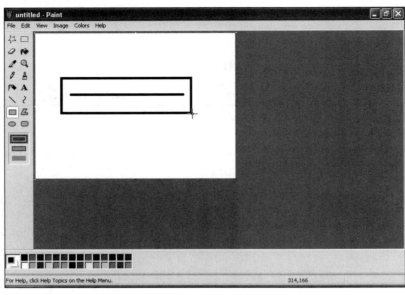

Exhibit 7-4: A sample Paint window

Do it!

A-3: Working with Paint

Here's how	Here's why
1 Click **Start**	
Choose **All Programs**, **Accessories**, **Paint**	To start Paint. A blank drawing area appears.
Maximize the window	Click the maximize button in the upper-right corner of the Paint window, if necessary.
2 Observe the toolbox	It's located along the left edge of the window. You can use these tools to create drawings and diagrams. By default, the pencil tool is selected.
3 Move the mouse into the drawing area	The shape of the mouse pointer changes to a pencil to help you draw freehand images.
While holding the mouse button, move the mouse	Notice that as you move the mouse, a line is drawn.
4 Choose **File**, **New**	To create a new drawing. A message box appears prompting you to save changes.
Click **No**	
5 In the toolbox, click	To activate the Line tool. A box containing various lines appears below the toolbox.
Observe the box	You can use the Line tool to draw straight lines of varying thickness. By default, the thinnest line is selected.

7–10   Introduction to Personal Computers

6 Click the thickest line

7 Move the mouse into the drawing area
The mouse pointer has changed to a crosshair to help you draw more precise lines.

8 Within the drawing area, click and hold the mouse button, then drag to draw a horizontal line, as shown

   Release the mouse button

9 Click
(In the toolbox.) To activate the Rectangle tool. Activating the Rectangle tool also changes the pointer to a crosshair.

   Drag the pointer diagonally to create a rectangle around the line, as shown

10 Choose **File**, **Exit**
To close Paint. A message box appears prompting you to save the changes.

   Click **No**
To close Paint without saving the drawing.

Topic B: Outlook Express

Explanation

E-mail is increasingly being used as a means of communication. Users send e-mail messages for both professional and personal purposes. One of the most popular applications that facilitates online communication is Outlook Express.

Components of the Outlook Express window

When you start Outlook Express for the first time, the Outlook Express startup window appears as shown in Exhibit 7-5.

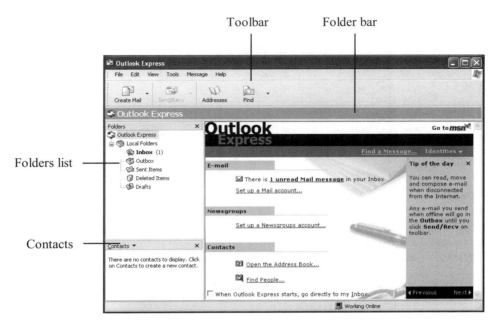

Exhibit 7-5: The Outlook Express startup window

The following table describes the components of the startup window.

Component	Description
Toolbar	Provides buttons to help create e-mail messages, send or receive messages, open the Address Book, and search for a message or details about a contact. The buttons on the toolbar change depending on the window that is open.
Folder bar	Displays the name of the folder that is selected.
Folders list	Displays a list of folders and subfolders that you can use to organize your messages. Some of the folders created by default are Inbox, Outbox, and Sent Items.
Contacts	Displays the names of the contacts in the Address Book.
Tip of the day	Displays a tip that helps you use various functions available in Outlook Express.

You can set the Inbox as the default window that opens when you start Outlook Express the next time. To do so, in the startup window, check When Outlook Express starts, go directly to my Inbox.

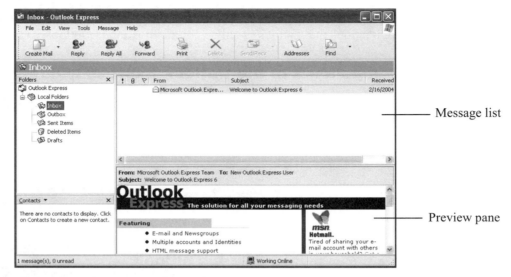

Exhibit 7-6: The message list and preview pane

Do it!

B-1: Examining the components of Outlook Express

Here's how	Here's why
1 Click **Start**	
Choose **All Programs, Outlook Express**	To start Outlook Express.
Maximize the window	Click the maximize button in the upper-right corner of the Outlook Express window, if necessary.
2 Observe the Toolbar	(As shown in Exhibit 7-5.) The toolbar consists of buttons that you can use instead of the menu commands. The buttons change depending on the folder that you select from the Folders list.
3 Observe the Folder bar	(As shown in Exhibit 7-5.) This bar displays the name of the folder that you open. Notice that it displays Outlook Express, indicating that the Outlook Express folder is open.

4	Observe the Folders list pane	It lists the folders created by default. The folders include local folders that have subfolders. You can add folders to this list.
	Click the indicated button	
		(If necessary.) To view the subfolders located in Local Folders. The default subfolders are Inbox, Outbox, Sent Items, Deleted Items, and Drafts.
5	In the Folders list, observe the subfolder Inbox	This subfolder has "(1)" next to it. This indicates that there is one unread message.
6	In the Folders list, click **Inbox**	The message list and Preview pane appear, as shown in Exhibit 7-6. The message list displays a list of messages in the Inbox and the Preview pane displays the content of the selected message.
7	In the Folders list, click **Outlook Express**	To return to the Outlook Express startup window.
8	Observe the Contacts pane	It displays the names of any contacts you have entered. Currently, no names have been entered as contacts.
9	Observe the Tip of the day pane	(On the right side of the Outlook Express startup window.) It displays a tip that will help you use the various functions available in Outlook Express. The tip changes every time you return to the Outlook Express startup window. You can also view other tips by clicking the Previous and Next buttons at the bottom of the Tip of the day pane.

7–14   Introduction to Personal Computers

Address Book

Explanation

The Address Book is one of the accessories available in Windows XP. You can store information about contacts, such as personal and professional details, create a mailing list for a group of contacts, and send and receive electronic business cards. You can also link directly to individual and business Internet addresses from the Address Book. In addition, you can search for addresses on the Internet.

You can open the Address Book in one of the following ways:

- Click Start, and then choose All Programs, Accessories, Address Book.
- In the Outlook Express window, on the toolbar, click the Addresses button.
- From the Outlook Express menu, choose Tools, Address Book.
- Press Ctrl+Shift+B.

Do it!

B-2: Using the Address Book in Outlook Express

Here's how	Here's why
1 Click [Addresses]	To open the Address Book – Main Identity window. You'll add a contact name to the Address Book.
Maximize the window	If necessary.
2 Click **New**	On the toolbar.
Observe the menu	New / Properties / New Contact... / New Group... / New Folder...
3 Choose **New Contact...**	To open the Properties dialog box. The Name tab is active by default. You'll enter details about the contact.
4 In the First box, type **Ruth**	Notice that as you type the name, the Display text box displays that name. This name will appear in the contacts list.
5 Press (TAB)	To move the insertion point to the Middle box.
In the Middle box, type **Mary**	
In the Last box, type **Baker**	Press Tab and then type Baker.
6 In the Title box, type **Ms**	
7 In the E-Mail Addresses box, type **ruthmary@aol.com**	

Working with applications   **7–15**

8 Click **Add**	The address is listed in the text area below the E-mail Addresses box. The text "Default E-Mail" next to the address indicates that it's set as the default e-mail address for this contact. If you had other addresses for this contact, you could set any one of them as the default address.
Click **OK**	To add this person to the Address Book and close the dialog box.
9 Observe the right pane	The details of the new contact appear in the Address Book list.
10 Choose **File**, **Exit**	To close the Address Book – Main Identity window and return to the Outlook Express startup window. Notice that the name of the newly added contact appears in the Contacts pane. You double-click the name to open the New Message window and send a message to this person.

7-16 Introduction to Personal Computers

Creating and sending e-mail messages

Explanation

Outlook Express helps you communicate with your friends and contacts by creating and sending e-mail messages. You create a new message in the New Message window. To open the New Message window, choose File, New, Mail Message, or click the Create Mail button.

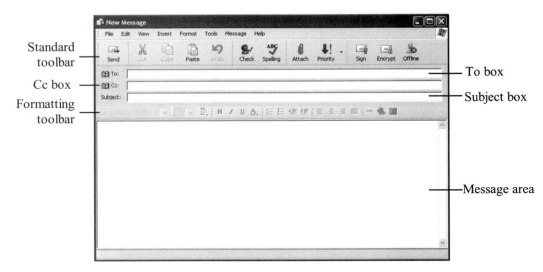

Exhibit 7-7: A New Message window

The following table describes the elements of a New Message window:

Element	Description
To box	The recipient's e-mail address is placed here. A recipient is the person who receives your e-mail message.
Cc box	The e-mail addresses of all the contacts you want to send a copy of the message to are placed here.
Subject box	A word or a phrase that describes the message contents is placed here.
Message area	The contents of the message are placed here.
Standard toolbar	Contains buttons for frequently used actions, such as sending messages and copying and moving text or graphics.
Formatting toolbar	Contains buttons that help you apply styles, fonts, and other character formats to your message text.

The Send/Recv button

The Send/Recv button is located on the Standard toolbar in the Outlook Express window. While Outlook will check for new e-mail messages at regular intervals, you can use this button to perform an immediate check for incoming messages. If there are any messages available at the time you click this button, they will be placed in your Inbox. This button will also send any messages that you might have in your Outbox.

Do it!

B-3: Creating and sending an e-mail message

Here's how	Here's why
1 Verify that Outlook Express is open	You'll create an e-mail message.
2 Click **Create Mail**	(On the Standard toolbar. You can also choose File, New, Mail Message or press Ctrl+N.) To open a New Message window.
Maximize the window	(If necessary.) The Standard and Formatting toolbars are near the top of the New Message window.
3 In the To box, type **Patconners@sitkabay.com**	This is the format of an e-mail address.
Press **TAB** twice	To move the insertion point to the Subject box. Notice that the Formatting toolbar becomes active when the insertion point is in the message area.
4 In the Subject box, type **Greetings from Park Ave**	This tells the recipient what your message is about.
5 Press **TAB**	To move the insertion point to the message area.
Type **The scenery is beautiful.**	
6 Observe **Send**	(The Send button is on the Standard toolbar.) You would use this button to send the message to Patconners@sitkabay.com.
7 Choose **File**, **Close**	To close the New Message window without sending the e-mail. A message box appears.
Click **No**	To close the message box without saving the e-mail.
8 In the Folders list, select **Inbox**	There are no new messages available at this time.
Observe **Send/Recv**	The Send/Recv button is on the Standard toolbar in the Outlook Express window.
9 Close Outlook Express	Click the Close button in the upper-right corner of the Outlook Express window.

7–18 Introduction to Personal Computers

Topic C: Internet Explorer 6.0

Explanation

The Internet has changed the way the world communicates. This is especially true in corporate environments, where e-mail and the World Wide Web (WWW) have become as indispensable as the telephone. The Internet connects homes, schools, libraries, government offices, hospitals, and commercial establishments where communication is an everyday activity. To access the Internet, you need a modem and a Web browser.

Modems

You can use a modem to connect your computer to any other computer in the world via telephone lines (also known as a dial-up modem connection) or cable TV networks. A modem (modulator demodulator) converts data on the computer into a form that can be transferred over telephone lines or cables. When receiving data, a modem converts incoming information into a form that a computer can interpret. You use modems for tasks such as sending e-mail messages, faxing, transferring files between computers, and exploring the Internet.

Modems are categorized based on the speed with which they transfer data. The speed of a modem is specified as bits per second (bps). It indicates the number of bits transferred in one second.

Internet Explorer 6.0

A *Web browser* is a software application that provides a graphical view of the Internet. Web browsers give you access to Web sites, which consist of Web pages. A Web page might contain text, graphics, animations, sounds, movies, and a variety of interactive elements. A Web browser makes it easy to navigate, or *surf*, the Web. A browser also makes it easy to copy information from the Web to your computer, a process known as *downloading*.

Internet Explorer 6.0 (IE 6) is one of the most popular Web browsers. To be able to use Internet Explorer to browse the Web, you must be connected to the Internet. When you are connected to the Internet, you are said to be *online*.

There are three ways to start Internet Explorer 6:

- Click Start, and then choose All Programs, Internet Explorer.
- Click the Internet Explorer icon on the Quick Launch bar (on the taskbar).
- Double-click the Internet Explorer icon on the desktop.

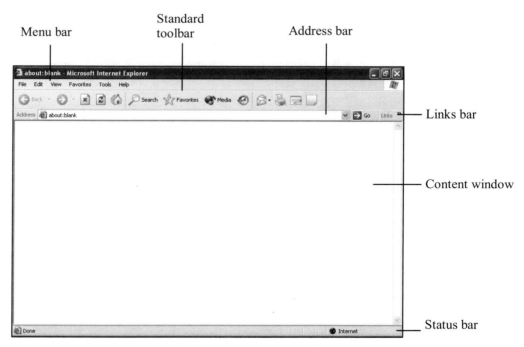

Exhibit 7-8: The components of the Internet Explorer 6 window

When Internet Explorer opens, you'll see that the browser interface (as shown in Exhibit 7-8) contains the standard Windows components: a title bar, a menu bar, a content window, and a status bar. It also includes a Standard toolbar and an Address bar similar to those in Windows Explorer and the My Computer window. This reflects Windows XP's Web integration design.

The Internet Explorer 6 toolbars

In addition to the Standard toolbar and the Address bar, Internet Explorer 6 includes a Links bar. Like the toolbars in other Windows programs, you can show, hide, resize, and arrange the toolbars to suit your work style.

The Standard toolbar (shown in Exhibit 7-9) provides buttons to facilitate navigation, searching, printing, and other common tasks. You can customize this toolbar to include other buttons such as Cut, Copy, and Paste, and you can delete any of the default buttons that you do not use very often.

Exhibit 7-9: The Standard toolbar

Introduction to Personal Computers

The Address bar (as shown in Exhibit 7-10) indicates the location of the Web page currently displayed in the content window. This location is also known as a *Uniform Resource Locator* (*URL*). You can think of a URL as the Internet address of a Web page. The Address bar also provides a drop-down list of recently visited sites. To access a Web page, type its URL in the Address bar and then click the Go button (or press the Enter key).

Exhibit 7-10: The Address bar

Do it!

C-1: Exploring the features of Internet Explorer 6.0

Here's how	Here's why
1 Click **Start** Choose **All Programs, Internet Explorer**	To start Internet Explorer.
Maximize the Internet Explorer window	If necessary.
2 Observe the content window	It displays a blank Web page. You can return to this page at any time by clicking the Home Page button on the Standard toolbar. You can specify a different Home Page to suit your needs.
3 Observe the Standard toolbar	In addition to the Home Page button, this toolbar provides context-sensitive buttons to help you surf the Web and perform other tasks such as printing and using e-mail.
4 Observe the Address bar	Address about:blank As you navigate to other Web pages, the Address bar will display the URL (or address) of each page.

Hyperlinks

Explanation

Before you start using Internet Explorer to surf the Web, it's helpful to learn about hyperlinks and URLs, which are the basic elements used for navigating in the Web environment.

Hyperlinks help you to navigate the Web by clicking words, icons, pictures, or other graphics on a Web page. When you point to a hyperlink, the mouse pointer changes to the shape of a hand. At the same time, the Internet Explorer status bar shows the URL associated with the hyperlink to which you are pointing.

Text-based hyperlinks are often underlined or displayed in a different color than the rest of the text on a Web page. Graphics-based hyperlinks can be icons, logos, buttons, and photographs.

Working with applications **7–21**

URLs and the Address bar

Clicking a hyperlink is one way to move to a specific URL. If you already know the URL of the Web page you want to visit, you can type it in the Address bar and then click the Go button (or press the Enter key).

Do it!

C-2: Using hyperlinks and the Address bar

Here's how	Here's why
1 In the Address bar, type **www.msn.com**	You'll browse the MSN Web site.
2 Click [→ Go]	(On the Address bar.) To access the MSN Web site.
3 Slowly move your mouse pointer over the MSN Web page	This will help you find the hyperlinks.
Observe the mouse pointer	When the pointer's shape changes to a hand, you know you're pointing to a hyperlink. Notice that hyperlinks can be text or graphics and that their appearance can change when you point to them. In some cases, pointing to a hyperlink displays other hyperlinks.
4 Observe the status bar	When you point to a hyperlink, its URL appears in the left side of the status bar.
5 Click any text hyperlink	The content window changes to display the associated Web page. Notice that the URL for the new page appears in the Address bar.
6 Click [← Back ▾]	(The Back button is on the Standard toolbar.) To go back to the MSN Web page.
7 Click [→ ▾]	(The Forward button is on the Standard toolbar.) To return to the Web page you chose in step 5.
8 Click any graphic hyperlink	The content window changes to display the associated Web page. Notice that the URL for the new page appears in the Address bar.
9 Experiment with the hypertext links	As you click the various links, observe the changes on your screen. You are "surfing" the Web. Your instructor will tell you when to end the activity.

7–22   Introduction to Personal Computers

Favorites

Explanation

A feature called Favorites in Internet Explorer can be used to store the URL of a Web page or a Web site. You can use Favorites to store the URLs of sites that you visit frequently. This feature eliminates the need to remember the URLs of different sites. You access Favorites by using either the menu bar or the toolbar.

Do it!

C-3:   Using Favorites

Here's how	Here's why
1 In the Address bar, type **www.google.com**	This is the URL for the Google Web site.
Click [→ Go]	To access the Google Web site.
2 Click [★ Favorites]	On the Standard toolbar.
Observe the Internet Explorer window	*[Favorites panel: Add... Organize... Hewlett-Packard Recommended... Links, MSN.com, Radio Station Guide]*
	The Internet Explorer window is divided into a left pane and a right pane. The left pane shows the Favorites explorer bar. The right pane shows the content of the Web page.
3 Click **Add**	*[Add Favorite dialog box: Internet Explorer will add this page to your Favorites list. OK, Make available offline, Customize..., Cancel, Name: Google, Create in >>]*
	(The Add button is on the Favorites explorer bar.) To open the Add Favorite dialog box.
Observe the Add Favorite dialog box	The Name box shows a title for the Web page.
4 Click **OK**	To add the URL of the Google Web site to the Favorites list.
Observe the left pane	The title Google appears in the Favorites list.
5 Click [🏠]	(On the Standard toolbar.) To return to your Home Page, which is a blank page.
6 In the left pane, click **Google**	To return to the Google Web site.
7 Close Internet Explorer	Click the Close button in the upper-right corner of the Internet Explorer window.

Topic D: Accessing Help and shutting down Windows XP

Explanation

Windows XP includes a Help program called Help and Support. It provides help topics on using Windows XP and troubleshooting problems with your computer. You can use Help and Support to search and learn about different features and tools available in Windows XP. It can also be used for getting online help and support from an online Microsoft support professional. For example, suppose you're working at home late in the evening. You need to print an important document that needs to be presented early the next morning at the office. However, when you print the document, the entire page is blank. You can use Windows Help and Support to find a solution to this problem.

To open the Help and Support Center window (as shown in Exhibit 7-11), click Start, and then choose Help and Support. The Help and Support Center window opens and functions in the same way as Internet Explorer. It contains the Standard toolbar, a Search bar, and a Content window. The Standard toolbar displays various buttons, such as Back, Forward, Home, Index, and Favorites. When you open the Help and Support Center window, the Help and Support Center home page appears in the Content window.

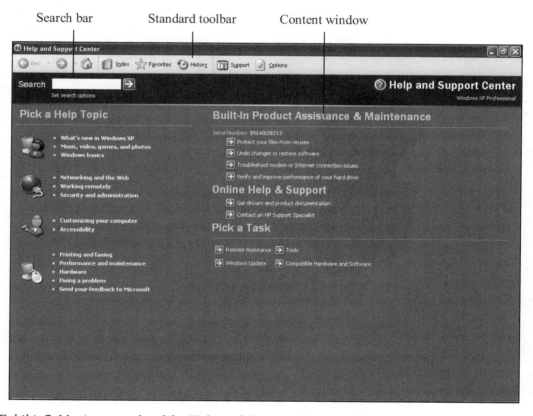

Exhibit 7-11: An example of the Help and Support Center window

7–24 Introduction to Personal Computers

Do it!

D-1: Exploring the features of Help and Support

Here's how	Here's why
1 Click **Start**	
Choose **Help and Support**	To open the Help and Support Center window.
2 Observe the Standard toolbar	It contains context-sensitive buttons that help you navigate the window and access Windows Help resources and online support.
3 Observe the Search bar	Search [_____] → Set search options It helps you search for information on a specific topic.
4 Observe the Content window	It provides hyperlinks to basic information related to Windows XP and your computer, troubleshooting tools, and external support resources. The hyperlinks on the left side of the Content window take you to commonly used help topics. The hyperlinks on the right side of the Content window take you to built-in and online help and support topics.

Search

Explanation

The Windows Help and Support Center provides a Search bar to help you locate assistance on a specific topic. By using the Search bar, you can view all Windows Help resources, including those available on the Internet. To use the Search bar, type a keyword or a phrase in the Search box, located below the Standard toolbar. Then, click the green arrow button or press Enter. The Content window then displays a list of help topics related to the keyword or phrase that you entered.

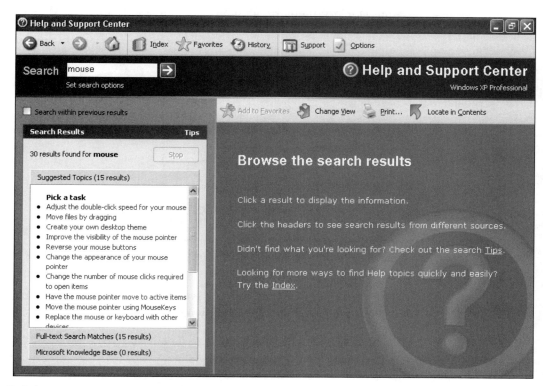

Exhibit 7-12: A sample of search results in the Help and Support Center window

Do it!

D-2: Using Search in Help and Support

Here's how	Here's why
1 In the Search box, type **mouse**	
Click	To start the search of the Help and Support Center.
Observe the Search Results list	An example is shown in Exhibit 7-12.
2 In the Search Results list, select **Reverse your mouse buttons**	To display detailed help on this subject.
Observe the Content window	It explains how to reverse the functions of your mouse buttons.
3 Close the Help and Support Center window	

The Shut Down Windows dialog box

Explanation

When you finish working on a computer, you should shut down, or turn off, that computer. You need to follow a procedure to shut down Windows XP properly to ensure the integrity of your data.

To shut down Windows XP correctly, you must use the Shut Down Windows dialog box. This ensures that you not only shut down Windows XP properly, but also that Windows XP will start properly the next time you switch on the computer. To open the Shut Down Windows dialog box (as shown in Exhibit 7-13), click Start and then click Shut Down.

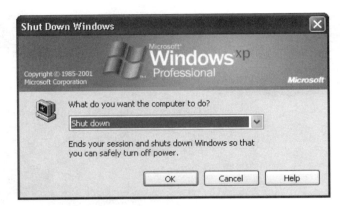

Exhibit 7-13: The Shut Down Windows dialog box

The Shut Down Windows dialog box provides five options. The most frequently used options are described in the following table.

Option	Description
Shut down	Ensures that all programs are closed and all unsaved information is saved before shutting down. Some computers are configured to automatically turn off the computer's power. For computers not configured this way, you'll see a message telling you that it's safe to turn off your computer. In either case, you must turn off the monitor yourself.
Restart	Ensures that all unsaved data is saved before the computer restarts. This procedure is also known as a "soft boot." If your computer takes longer than usual to perform tasks or experiences quirky or intermittent problems, you can try solving such problems by restarting the computer.

If you're using a computer that is not part of a network domain (the computer is not connected to other computers), you might not have the Shut Down option. Instead, you'll have an option called *Turn off computer*, which performs the same function as the Shut Down procedure. To turn off your computer, click Start, and then click Turn Off Computer. In the Turn off computer dialog box, click Turn Off.

Do it!

D-3: Shutting down your computer

Here's how	Here's why
1 Close all the open applications	If necessary.
2 Remove the floppy disk from its drive	If necessary.
3 Click **Start**	
Click [⏻ Shut Down]	The Shut Down Windows dialog box appears (as shown in Exhibit 7-13.)
4 Display the Shut down list	Shut down ⌄ Click the down-arrow.
5 Observe the choices	The Shut down list provides various options. The Shut down option turns off your computer. The Restart option turns off your computer and then restarts it.
6 Click **Cancel**	To close the Shut Down Windows dialog box.

7–28 Introduction to Personal Computers

Unit summary: Working with applications

Topic A   In this topic, you learned how to use Windows XP Accessories: **WordPad**, **Calculator**, and **Paint**.

Topic B   In this topic, you learned about the components of **Outlook Express** and how to use the **Address Book** in Outlook Express. You also learned how to create and send an **e-mail message**.

Topic C   In this topic, you used Microsoft's Web browser, **Internet Explorer**, to access the Internet and add a URL to the **Favorites** list.

Topic D   In this topic, you learned how to access Windows **Help and Support** and **shut down** and **restart** a computer.

Independent practice activity

1 Use Calculator to calculate the sum of **520** and **450**. Then, multiply the sum by **50**. (*Hint*: The result should be 48500.)

2 Using Paint, draw a square with a diagonal, as shown in Exhibit 7-14.

3 Close Paint. You don't need to save the Paint file.

4 In the Address Book for Outlook Express, add contact information (name, e-mail address) for a friend.

5 Close the Address Book.

6 Start Internet Explorer.

7 Access the CNN Web site, **www.cnn.com**.

8 Add **www.cnn.com** to Favorites.

9 Close Internet Explorer.

10 Open the Help and Support Center window.

11 Search for help on a subject of your choice.

12 Close all the open applications.

13 Shut down your computer.

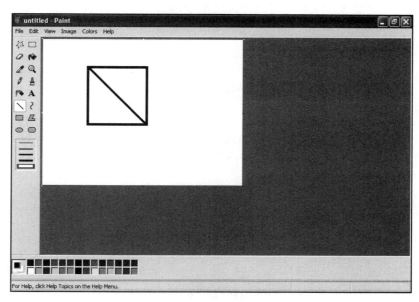

Exhibit 7-14: After step 2, the Paint window should look like this

Review questions

1 Which of the following is not one of the Windows XP accessories?

   A WordPad

   B WinZip

   C Paint

   D Calculator

2 When using the word processor accessory, how do you change the appearance of the text?

3 In Paint, how many drawings can you have open at the same time?

4 Why would you use Outlook Express?

5 Why is it important to enter text in the Subject box?

7–30 Introduction to Personal Computers

6 Name one way to start Internet Explorer.

7 Which of the following helps you to navigate the Web by clicking words, icons, pictures, or other graphics on a Web page?

A Hyperlink

B Address bar

C URL

D Favorites

8 Why is it important to properly shut down your Windows XP computer when you are finished working?

Course summary

This summary contains information to help you bring the course to a successful conclusion. Using this information, you will be able to:

A Use the summary text to reinforce what you've learned in class.

B Determine the next courses in this series (if any), as well as any other resources that might help you continue to learn about personal computers.

S–2   Introduction to Personal Computers

Topic A: Course summary

Use the following summary text to reinforce what you've learned in class.

Unit summaries

Unit 1

In this unit, you learned about the **evolution** of computers and about various types of computers. You also learned about the benefits and limitations of computers, uses of **personal computers**, and about **desktops** and **portables**. Next, you learned about the **Input-Process-Output** cycle that a computer uses. You also learned about **hardware**, **software**, and types of **operating systems**. Finally, you learned what happens when you switch on a computer, and you also identified various **desktop components**.

Unit 2

In this unit, you learned how to use the most common input devices, the **mouse** and the **keyboard**. You also learned about other input devices, such as **a mouse with a wheel button**, **light pens**, **touch screens**, **trackballs**, **joysticks**, **scanners**, **pen input/digitizing tablets**, **touch pads**, **digital cameras**, **Optical Character Recognition**, **Optical Mark Reader**, and **microphones**.

Unit 3

In this unit, you learned about the components of a **system unit**. You also learned that the **central processing unit (CPU)** processes data and performs tasks in response to the requests of peripheral devices. Then, you learned that **random access memory (RAM)** is a temporary storage area that stores data and instructions required by the microprocessor to perform a task. You also learned that **read-only memory (ROM)** stores **firmware** permanently.

Unit 4

In this unit, you learned how to **write-protect** and **format** a **floppy disk**. Next, you learned about **hard disks** and how to check the capacity of a hard disk. You also learned about the other storage devices, such as **CD-ROMs, DVDs, Click disks, keydrives, SuperDisks, Zip disks, Optical disks, Magnetic strips, Smart cards, portable hard drives**, and **rewritable CDs**.

Unit 5

In this unit, you learned about the different types of **monitors** and their features. You also learned how to set **desktop backgrounds** and **screensavers**. Next, you learned that **printers** are used to obtain printed copies of documents. You also learned that **plotters** are used to print high-quality prints. Finally, you learned about **sound card** basics.

Unit 6

In this unit, you learned that **files** and **folders** are organized in a folder hierarchy—with C: as the root folder. Then, you learned how to navigate the folder hierarchy by using **Windows Explorer**. You also learned how to **create** and **rename** a folder and how to **save, print, move, copy, delete, restore,** and **search** files. Finally, you learned how to protect their computer against **viruses**.

Course summary **S–3**

Unit 7

In this unit, you learned how to use the Windows XP Accessories **WordPad**, **Calculator**, and **Paint**. Next, you learned about the components of the **Outlook Express** window and how to use the **Address Book** in Outlook Express. You also learned how to create and send an **e-mail message**. Next, you learned how to work with **Internet Explorer 6.0**. Finally, you learned how to access **Help and Support** and **shut down** a computer.

S–4   Introduction to Personal Computers

Topic B: Continued learning after class

It is impossible to learn to use any software effectively in a single day. To get the most out of this class, you should begin working with personal computers (PCs) to perform real tasks as soon as possible. Course Technology also offers resources for continued learning.

Next courses in this series

This is the only course in this series.

Other resources

You might find some of these other resources useful as you continue to learn about PCs. For more information, visit www.course.com.

- *Computer Concepts – Illustrated Complete*
  ISBN: 0-619-10909-2

- *A Record of Discovery for Exploring Computers, Fourth Edition*
  ISBN: 0-7895-6372-X

- *Essential Introduction to Computers*
  ISBN: 0-619-20078-2

Introduction to Personal Computers

Quick reference

Button	Shortcut keys	Function
Search		Opens the "Search Companion" Search feature in Windows Explorer
B	CTRL + B	Makes the selected text bold
I	CTRL + I	Italicizes the selected text
U	CTRL + U	Underlines the selected text
		Applies various colors to selected text in WordPad
		Left aligns the selected text
		Centers the selected text
		Right aligns the selected text
		Converts the selected text to a bulleted list
	CTRL + S	Updates a file
		Activates the Line tool in Paint
		Activates the Rectangle tool in Paint

Q–2   Introduction to Personal Computers

Button	Shortcut keys	Function
Addresses	CTRL + SHIFT + B	Opens the Address Book in Outlook Express
Create Mail	CTRL + N	Creates a new e-mail message in Outlook Express
Send	ALT + S	Sends an e-mail message in Outlook Express
Send/Recv	CTRL + M	Checks for new messages in Outlook Express
Go	↵ ENTER	Opens a new Web page in Internet Explorer
Back	ALT + ←	Moves to the previous Web page in Internet Explorer
(forward)	ALT + →	Moves to the next Web page in Internet Explorer
Favorites		Opens the Favorites explorer bar
(home)	ALT + HOME	Returns to the Home Page
(close)	ALT + F4	Closes an application

Glossary

Address Book
A Windows XP accessory that is used to store information about contacts, create a mailing list for a group of contacts, and send and receive electronic business cards.

Application software
Software that is designed for specific purposes such as creating documents, browsing the Internet, and accounting.

Arithmetic-Logic Unit (ALU)
The part of the CPU that executes the computer operation.

Backup
A copy of a file that is stored in a different location than the original file.

Binary digit (bit)
The smallest unit of information for a computer. The value of a bit can be 1 or 0.

Booting
A process that the operating system automatically begins which starts the computer.

Byte
A group of eight bits. Memory is measured in terms of bytes.

CD-ROM (Compact Disc Read-Only Memory)
A removable storage device that can store a large amount of information.

Central Processing Unit (CPU)
A set of electronic components that interprets the data you enter, processes it, and generates the output. (Also known as the *microprocessor*.)

Click disk
A removable storage device that is used in digital cameras or notebook computers.

Clicking
Pressing and releasing the left mouse button.

Color monitors
A monitor that can display hundreds to millions of colors.

Computer
A machine that you use to store and manipulate information.

Control unit
The part of the CPU that directs the flow of instructions to be executed.

Desktop
In Windows XP, it contains programs (also called applications) that you use to perform tasks such as creating and editing documents, working with storage devices, and printing documents.

Digital camera
A camera that you use to take photographs that can be transferred to a computer without scanning them.

Dot pitch
The distance between two pixels. As the dot pitch decreases, the sharpness of the text or image displayed increases.

Dot matrix printer
Produces low-quality print as compared to laser and inkjet printers. It's the oldest of the three types of printers.

Double-clicking
Pressing and releasing the left mouse button twice in rapid succession.

Downloading
Copying information from the Web to your computer.

Dragging
Holding down the left mouse button while moving the mouse pointer. (Also called *drag and drop*.)

Drum plotter
The paper is wrapped around a drum and anchored at both ends. The drum rotates while the pen moves laterally.

DVDs (Digital Video Devices)
A storage device that stores the same type of information as CD-ROMs. However, DVDs can store much more data than CD-ROMs.

Expansion slots
A set of sockets that you use to attach additional input and output devices to your computer. You can also use these slots to add more memory.

File
The basic unit of storage on a computer.

G–2   Introduction to Personal Computers

Firmware

The computer's essential software that is stored in ROM chips.

Flatbed plotter

The paper is held stationary while the pen moves over it.

Floppy disk drive

A storage device that is used to store small amounts of information. They are removable and suitable for transferring data from one computer to another.

Folder

The organizational method that is used to store files on your computer.

Formatting

(1) The process of checking the disk for bad sectors and then allocating tracks and sectors on the recording area. (2) Changing the appearance of a document's contents.

Hard disk

A storage device inside the system unit that's used to store large amounts of data.

Hard disk drive

A self-contained box that houses the hard disk.

Hardware

A computer's physical components, and are used during all three phases of the I-P-O cycle

Host

A file that a virus copies itself into and then creates multiple copies of itself on different locations of the hard disk.

Hyperlinks

Used to navigate the Web by clicking words, icons, pictures, or other graphics on a Web page.

Icons

Pictorial representations of the programs or applications.

Infrared port

Allows two computers or a computer and a device to communicate without the use of wires.

Inkjet printer

Produces high quality print but is slow in performance. It's available in either color or black-and-white and costs less than a laser printer.

Input devices

Hardware that is used to input data into the computer. Common devices include keyboards, mouse, trackballs, joysticks, scanners, pen-input or digitizing tablets, touch pads, and digital cameras.

Input-Process-Output (I-P-O)

A principle that characterizes most production processes. Computers accept the data you enter as input, process it, and then produce information as output.

Insertion point

A flashing vertical line on the screen indicates the position where you can start typing the characters.

Interpersonal computing era

A period of time that is characterized by networks of interconnected computers that organizations, schools, and homes use for communication and data storage and manipulation.

Internet era

A period of time that is characterized by the development of Internet technology, which has revolutionized the way people work and communicate. (Can also be another name for the interpersonal computing era)

Institutional computing era

A period of time that is characterized by a few large and expensive computers that were used to meet the data processing requirements of large organizations, government agencies, and scientific and military establishments.

Joystick

A lever that can move in all directions, controlling a pointer or some other symbol on a monitor. This device is commonly used to play video or multimedia games.

Keyboard

An input device used for entering letters, numbers, and other characters; you can also use the keyboard to navigate menus and run commands.

Keydrive

A removable storage device that is used to transfer large amounts of data, for example, between home and office. Ideal for use in laptops; similar in size to a small key ring. (Also called a USB flash drive.)

Laptop

A portable computer with the same computing power as a desktop but weighs much less and has a built-in video screen.

Laser printer

Produces high quality output, both in text and graphics, is available in either color or black-and-white, and costs more than an inkjet printer.

Light pen

A device similar to a pen that you use to select an option on the screen by pointing to it. You can also use a light pen to draw an image by sketching it directly on the monitor.

Glossary **G-3**

Loading
The process where the data and instructions that are to be used are moved from the hard disk to RAM.

Magnetic strip
A removable storage device that is used to store small amounts of information such as the personal identity number on a credit card.

Mainframe
A large and expensive multi-user computer on which hundreds of users can work simultaneously on the same data. Mainframes have large data storage capacity and can process bulk data.

Memory
Tiny electronic circuits that store data for processing. It is the internal memory of a computer present on the motherboard. The amount of memory a computer has is measured in kilobytes, megabytes, and gigabytes.

Microphone
A device that converts sound into electrical signals. This device is commonly used for two-way audio communication on the Internet

Microprocessor
A component inside the system unit that processes input and generates output. (Also known as the *CPU*.)

Minicomputer
A multi-user computer that can support 4 to 200 users simultaneously.

Modem (modulator demodulator)
A communication device that allows you to access the Internet. To use a modem, you need communication software that allows your computer to interact with the device.

Monitor
A video screen that displays the user interface of the active software program(s).

Monochrome monitors
A monitor that can display only two colors, one for the foreground and the other for the background.

Motherboard
A large board inside the system unit that houses the CPU and other components. All the input/output devices are connected to the motherboard.

Mouse
An input device used for pointing to and selecting options; moving the mouse moves an arrowhead pointer on the monitor.

Mouse pointer
A pointing arrow that appears and moves on the screen as you move the mouse.

Multiprocessing
Running a program on multiple microprocessors (CPUs), leading to an increase in the processing speed.

Multitasking
Simultaneously running multiple programs.

Notebook
A computing device with the same processing power as a laptop but is much smaller.

Notification area
In Windows XP, it contains a clock and displays the status of specific programs and controls.

Number crunching
Performing arithmetic and comparison operations quickly.

Operating System (OS)
Software that carries out the basic functions of a computer. The operating system provides an environment for hardware and software to work together. Common operating systems include Windows XP, Macintosh, and UNIX.

Optical Character Recognition (OCR)
A device that you use to recognize each character in a photographic image of printed or handwritten text. This device is commonly used to read bar codes or sort letters at post offices by reading postal codes.

Optical disk
A removable storage device that is used to store large picture files and photographs in a digital camera.

Optical Mark Reader (OMR)
A device that scans pencil marks by using infrared light. This device is commonly used to scan answer sheets for multiple-choice questions or lottery tickets.

Outlook Express
A Windows XP email program that is used for online communication.

Paint
A graphics program that is available with Windows XP.

Palmtop
A device that you can hold in the palm of your hand. Palmtops, such as PalmPilots, are among the smallest of all the portables, usually the size of a pocket calculator. You can use palmtops only for limited, built-in applications.

Panes
One of two sections in Windows Explorer.

G–4   Introduction to Personal Computers

Path

The location of a file or a folder in which the name of the root folder, other folders, subfolders, and the file are separated by back slashes (\). (Also called the *address*.)

Pen input/digitizing tablets

A set consisting of an electronic pen and an electromagnetic tablet that you can use as high-tech drawing tools. These tools are suitable for drawing high-quality sketches, tracing intricate patterns, and performing photo restoration.

Personal Computer (PC)

A small, single-user computer that you can use to perform a variety of tasks, ranging from maintaining household finances to managing the finances of a large company.

Personal computing era

A period of time that was characterized by small and inexpensive microcomputers.

Personal Digital Assistant (PDA)

A handheld device originally designed as a personal organizer. It includes a clock, a date book, an address book, a task list, a memo pad, and a simple calculator.

Pixels (picture elements)

An array of tiny dots that are displayed on a monitor screen.

Platter

A disk that is divided into tracks and sectors. A personal computer might contain up to eight platters.

Plotter

An output device that uses a pen to print output on large sheets of paper. It produces continuous lines unlike a printer, which simulates lines by printing a series of dots. Plotters are used to print high-quality visuals, charts, graphs, tables, and diagrams.

Pointing

Positioning the mouse pointer over an object.

Ports

An interface to which you connect a device. There are three types of ports: serial, parallel, and USB.

Primary mouse button

By default, the left mouse button.

Printer

An output device used for transferring output to paper.

Quick Launch toolbar

In Windows XP, it's used to display the desktop, launch Internet Explorer (an application used to access the Internet), or launch Windows Media Player (an application used to play digital media).

Random access memory (RAM)

The memory that stores data and instructions temporarily; that is, while the computer is switched on.

Read-only memory (ROM)

Memory that can be read but not changed. It is sometimes referred to as nonvolatile storage because its contents remain in storage even when the power is switched off.

Recycle Bin

A folder located on the hard disk that temporarily stores files and folders that have been deleted. To permanently remove the files, you must empty the Recycle Bin.

Resolution

The number of pixels that appear on the screen.

Rewritable CD (CD-RW)

A removable storage device that is used to record and re-record data on the same CD-ROM.

Right-clicking

Pressing and releasing the right mouse button.

Root folder

The folder at the top of the hierarchy in a storage device, such as a hard disk or a floppy disk.

Scanner

A device that you use to copy an existing image and store it on your computer.

Screensaver

A utility that displays text or graphics on the screen when your computer is idle for a specified time. Pressing a key or moving the mouse deactivates the screensaver.

Server

A computer that makes programs and data available to a network of computers. It also handles communication between interconnected computers. Servers can also be used as multi-user computers.

Smart card

A removable storage device that is used to store information such as phone numbers and phone settings, and processing information to generate the necessary output.

Glossary **G–5**

Software

Sets of instructions that a computer requires to perform various tasks, such as managing hardware components, creating a document, and sending e-mail messages. There are two categories of software, system and application.

Sound card

A commonly used output device that helps you obtain sound output on speakers attached to your computer.

Start button

In Windows XP, it's used to start applications, get help, configure the computer, and shut down your computer.

Storage capacity

The amount of information a disk can store, and the number of tracks and sectors determines it.

Subfolder

A folder stored within another folder.

Supercomputer

A very fast computer that can process billions of instructions per second. Supercomputers are used to perform tasks that involve processing large amounts of data, and processing tasks with complex requirements such as weather forecasting, biomedical applications, and aircraft design.

System software

Controls hardware components such as the mouse, the keyboard, and the computer's memory. System software consists of an operating system and basic utility software, such as device controller software.

System unit

A box that contains various electronic components and circuitry required to run a computer

Tablet PC

A computer that looks like a notebook. It has a screen on which a user can write with a special purpose pen.

Taskbar

In Windows XP, the area located at the bottom of the screen. It contains the Start button, the Quick Launch toolbar, and the notification area.

Touch pad

A stand-alone pointing device on which you tap gently to move around on the desktop.

Touch screen

A monitor that makes it easier for you to select an option by pointing to it with your finger.

Tracks

A series of concentric circles that divides the storage area on a floppy disk. Tracks are further divided into sectors. Both are numbered, which makes it easier to write and locate data stored on a disk.

Trackball

A pointing device with a ball resting within a case (similar to an inverted mouse). Trackballs are used with portable computers.

Uniform Resource Locator (URL)

The Internet address of a Web page that appears in the Address bar.

Updating

Saving an existing document with the same name in the same location. This action does not require you to interact with the Save As dialog box.

Virus

A set of instructions (a program) that is designed to interrupt the operations of a computer or damage the data and programs on it.

Wearable computer

A small personal computer that users can wear while operating. This device is being developed and designed to act as an intelligent assistant.

Web browser

Software application that provides a graphical view of the Internet. Web browsers give you access to Web sites, which consist of Web pages. A Web page might contain text, graphics, animations, sounds, movies, and a variety of interactive elements.

WordPad

A Windows XP accessory that is a simple and efficient word processor.

Write-protecting

Preventing files from being deleted or changed on a floppy disk by sliding the write-protect tab on the disk to the open position.

Zip disk

A removable storage device that is used to transfer large amounts of data between computers.

G–6   Introduction to Personal Computers

Index

A

Address Book, 7-14
Addresses, 6-2
Application software, 1-12, G-1
Arithmetic-logic unit (ALU), 3-4

B

Backups, 6-15
Binary digits (bits), 3-6
Booting, 1-15
Bytes, 3-6, G-1

C

Calculator, 7-7
CD-Recorders, 4-10
CD-ROMs, 4-10
Central processing unit (CPU), 3-2, 3-4
Color monitors, 5-2, G-1
Computers
    Benefits and limitations, 1-5
    Defined, 1-2, G-1
    Evolution of, 1-2
    Multiuser, 1-2, G-3
    Types of, 1-2
Control unit, 3-4

D

Desktop components, 1-15
Dot pitch, 5-2
Downloading from the Web, 7-18
Drag and drop, 2-2
DVD recorders, 4-10
DVDs, 4-10, G-1

E

E-mail messages, 7-16
Extensions, 6-8

F

Files, 6-2
    Backups, 6-15
    Copying to floppy disks, 6-15
    Creating, 6-8
    Defined, 6-2
    Deleting, 6-16
    Extensions, 6-8

Moving, 6-14
    Printing, 6-12
    Restoring, 6-17
    Saving, 6-8
    Searching for, 6-18
    Updates, 6-9
Firmware, 3-7
Floppy disks
    Copying files to, 6-15
    Formatting, 4-3
    Sectors, 4-3, G-5
    Storage capacity, 4-3
    Tracks, 4-3, G-5
    Write-protecting, 4-2
Folders
    Creating, 6-6
    Defined, 6-2
    Naming, 6-6
    Renaming, 6-7
    Subfolders, 6-2
Formatting floppy disks, 4-3

H

Hard disks
    Capacity, 4-8
    Comparison with floppy disks, 4-6
    Defined, 4-6
    Platters, 4-6
Hardware, 1-8
    Components, 1-10
Help and Support feature, 7-23
Host files, 6-20
Hyperlinks, 7-20, 7-30

I

Icons, 1-15
Input devices, 1-10, 2-7
Input-Process-Output (I-P-O) cycle, 1-8
Insertion point, 2-4
Internet era, 1-2

K

Keyboard keys, 2-5

L

Loading, 3-6

I–2 Introduction to Personal Computers

M

Memory
  Defined, 3-6
  Random access memory (RAM), 3-6, G-4
  Read-only memory (ROM), 3-7, G-4
Microprocessors, 1-8
Modems, 7-18
Monitors
  Color, 5-2, G-3
  Monochrome, 5-2, G-3
Monochrome monitors, 5-2, G-3
Motherboard, 3-2
Mouse
  Defined, 2-2
  Operations, 2-2
Multiuser computers, 1-2, G-3

N

Notification area, 1-15, G-5
Number crunching, 3-4

O

Online, 7-18
Operating systems, 1-14, G-3
Outlook Express, 7-11

P

Paint, 7-8
Panes, 6-3
Paths, 6-2
Personal computers (PCs)
  Defined, 1-2, 1-3
  Desktops, 1-6
  Portable, 1-6
  Uses, 1-6
Pixels, 5-2, G-4
Platters, 4-6
Plotters, 5-8, G-4
Pointer, 2-2
Primary mouse button, 2-2
Printer types, 5-7

Q

Quick Launch toolbar, 1-15, G-5

R

Random access memory (RAM), 3-6, G-4
Read-only memory (ROM), 3-7, G-4
Recycle Bin, 6-8
Resolution, 5-2, 5-10
Root folder, 6-2

S

Scanning, 2-8
Screensavers, 5-5, G-4
Search Companion, 6-18
Sectors, 4-3, G-5
Shut Down Windows dialog box
  Opening, 7-26
Software
  Application, 1-12, G-1
  Defined, 1-8
  Firmware, 3-7
  Operating systems, 1-14, G-3
  System, 1-12, G-5
Sound cards, 1-10, 5-9, G-5
start button, 1-15, G-5
Storage capacity, 4-3
Subfolders, 6-2
Surfing the Web, 7-18
System software, 1-12, G-5
System unit components, 3-2

T

Taskbar, 1-15
Tracks, 4-3, G-5

U

Uniform Resource Locators (URLs), 7-20
Updates, 6-9

V

Viruses, 6-20

W

Web browsers, 7-18, G-5
Windows Explorer panes, 6-3
WordPad
  Editing documents, 7-3
  Formatting documents, 7-3
Write-protecting floppy disks, 4-2